THE
COLLECTOR'S ENCYCLOPEDIA OF

Homer Laughlin

CHINA

REFERENCE & VALUE GUIDE

Joanne Jasper

COLLECTOR BOOKS
A Division Of Schroeder Publishing Co., Inc.

Searching For A Publisher?

We are always looking for knowledgeable people considered experts within their fields. If you feel that there is a need for a book on your collectible subject and have a comprehensive collection, contact us.

COLLECTOR BOOKS
P.O. Box 3009
Paducah, Kentucky 42002-3009

ACKNOWLEDGMENTS

While visiting my oldest daughter in Washington DC, a visit she and I took to the Homer Laughlin Factory in Newell, West Virginia set in motion the idea that this book could become a reality. This is due in part to the very friendly and helpful reception I received from Mr. Dave Conley and Mr. Joe Wells III. During later visits, Mr. Joseph Wells, Jr. and Mr. Bob Wells were good enough to answer my many questions and help in other ways. (Mr. Joseph Wells, Jr. came to my rescue when I was there on a Saturday and became convinced that I was locked in the second floor showroom.)

Bob Jones of the Homer Laughlin family gave me extra time, not only answering questions and acting as escort but even helping set up tables to take china pictures. Jonathan Parry, the current art director, put up with my invading his rooms and digging into his books. Many thanks to the others at the Homer Laughlin factory, who were contributors in their own way.

Donna Juszczak at the East Liverpool Museum of Ceramics was tireless in her help to get me copies of many of the old trade magazines and Homer Laughlin catalogs that appear in this book. If you get a chance to visit the Museum of Ceramics, it is well worth the extra trip.

Mr. Ed Carson, who is mentioned in so many other Collector Books in connection with Homer Laughlin, also contributed copies of pictures from his collection, commented on my writing and helped obtain information. I consider him a good friend.

I owe a great deal to Darlene Nossaman, a Homer Laughlin historian in her own right, who contributed information, china for photographs, pictures of some of the larger sets of her 3,000 plus collection, and encouragement (and emergency shipments of china) on an almost weekly basis.

My thanks to Mr. Don Schreckengost, not only for all the information that he gave to me but for the thrill of interviewing one of the people who made some of the special history happen at Homer Laughlin. His credentials as a designer of china are very impressive.

For assistance in the compilation of the value guide, I am indebted to Dr. David Long of the School for Appraisers, who graciously welcomed me into his home and spent a Sunday afternoon explaining to me some of the mysteries and arts of valuing antique china.

The Corning Museum of Glass in Corning, New York and the reference department of the Reseda Branch of the Los Angeles Public Library made it possible for me to examine what must have been miles of microfilm of old trade publications, some of whose pages are reproduced in this book.

The photography proved to be an almost insurmountable task. My thanks to the people at the Westlake Photo Lab, who finally made it possible to obtain pictures that looked just like the dishes.

Harvey Duke, Jack Chipman and Lois Lehner, whose books I have gone through so many times, gave me words of encouragement and in Ms. Lehner's case copies of some old advertisements of early Homer Laughlin shapes.

Lastly my greatest aid came from my husband John, who acted as co-author for many pages in this book. Just to live with me as I came home each night from my regular job and poured myself into my picture taking, writing or research would require the patience of a saint. He has helped me search for china in many antique stores (looking for first blood, as he calls it), carted me to libraries all over the Los Angeles area, entered data, edited my work and added to the history of Homer Laughlin some of his own interesting ideas.

TABLE OF CONTENTS

INTRODUCTION

During the past 100 years, a vital revolution took place in the American dinnerware industry. In the late 1880's America was dependent upon imports (especially from England) for its fine dinnerware. In 1871 Homer Laughlin took on the challenge of making American china which would rival that imported from England. This marked the founding of Homer Laughlin China, which was to grow to become the largest potter in the world. During the first half of the twentieth century, the Homer Laughlin China Company developed a multitude of different china shapes, which appeared on millions of dinner tables throughout America. In the 1960's the emphasis of HLC production began to change from china for home use to institutional china. Today a mere shadow of the fabulous output of this pottery may be found in the antiques stores and in private collections. This book documents what may be considered the heyday of HLC home dinnerware, the period from 1900 to 1950.

The purpose of this book is twofold. For the casual collector of HLC china, this book will show the evolution of the HLC designs through the years. It illustrates, with many examples, the beautiful designs produced by Frederick Rhead, Don Schreckengost, and other art directors who transformed the HLC pottery styles from those which imitated European designs to those that were uniquely American, and which mirrored the changes in tastes over the years. This book provides a quick journey in time from the days when automobiles were a curiosity until the postwar years when Japanese china imports began to displace American china on the shelves of retailers. For this reason I have listed the china shapes chronologically instead of alphabetically.

For the serious collector and dealer, this book is intended to be a reference manual which can assist in the identification of different shapes and decorative patterns. It is especially intended to assist in differentiating between shapes which closely resemble one another. The book also provides specific identifications for many of the decorative patterns found on HLC china, although the total number of patterns shown here can be no more than a drop in the bucket compared to the fifteen or so new patterns for *each different shape* that was shown at each china show where prospective customers could see the new wares. In the appendices will be found a price guide as well as other interesting and helpful information.

The Homer Laughlin China Company was launched, not surprisingly by a man named Homer Laughlin, who, together with his brother, Shakespeare, built a small pottery in East Liverpool, Ohio in 1871. The choice of location was probably due to the proximity of clays, which produced a type of pottery known as "yellow ware," from the bright yellow color of the fired ware. Unfortunately, yellow ware was not a very suitable vehicle for the display of decorations and was certainly not to be associated with better class dining.

In 1872 the city fathers of East Liverpool raised a $5,000.00 prize, to induce a potter to establish a plant for the making of white ware. The Laughlin brothers took advantage of the offer and built a two-kiln plant for making this type of pottery. From a trade publication of 1938, we learned that the populace of East Liverpool initially had cause to regret their funding of the Laughlin brothers. When the first batch of the new china was removed from the kilns, the handles dropped off all the cups. These problems were eventually corrected, and the new operation became a success.

By the fall of 1874, the company was known as "Ohio Valley Pottery" and employed over 100 workers. Two years later in 1876 they received the highest award at the Centennial Exposition at Philadelphia for their white ware. One would not like to imply that this achievement was simple. As will be explained later, the making of fine china is very much an art, and the Laughlin brothers did not master this instantly. However, by 1886 they had demonstrated the capability to make fine china which displayed the attribute of translucence, an important characteristic of vitreous china.

Having acquired the capability to make true china, Homer Laughlin did not hesitate to exploit this fact. Previously, fine china had to be imported especially from England. Homer Laughlin symbolized his taking on of the English pottery industry by his early back stamp: An eagle attacking a lion, which was lying helplessly on its back, symbolizing the ascendancy of the American pottery industry over the English.

In 1897 Homer Laughlin, having twenty years previously bought out the interest of his brother Shakespeare, sold out completely to a group headed by Louis I. Aaron and his sons Marcus Aaron and Charles I. Aaron. Mr. Louis Aaron assumed responsibility for the presidency of the company and for its financial affairs, and Mr. W. E. Wells, as General Manager, took over responsibility for the operation of the plant. Under this management the company prospered greatly and launched on a career of producing truly enormous quantities of china for America's tables. The Aaron and Wells families have continued in their respective roles through four generations, until the present day.

The next advances were to occur in the production and design of the china itself. In the area of china production Dr. Albert Bleininger, who was regarded by some as the leading ceramics engineer in the world, joined HLC in 1920. He came there from the U.S. Bureau of Standards in Pittsburgh. In 1934 he was joined by Harry Thiemecke, who retired from the company in 1972. Mr. Thiemecke told me in a telephone interview that he was attracted to HLC by the opportunity to work with Dr. Bleininger. Together these men devised the formulas for clays and glazes and the manufacturing methods that produced the beautiful pieces seen in this book.

In 1927 Mr. Frederick Rhead came to HLC as the art director. Prior to his joining the company, the designs of the different shapes appear to have been farmed out to various local free-lance designers. For the most part, the designs from the pre-Rhead period tended to imitate those of the European potteries. Rhead's arrival initiated an outpouring of new designs. Starting slowly at first with **Newell**, which was not a popular shape, he next created **Liberty**, which was actually derived from **Newell**. He then began to make his presence more strongly felt with **Century** (1931), making a sharp break with the past. Century is a rectilinear shape reminiscent of Art Deco, and its ivory-like glaze is unmistakable. While Rhead is perhaps best known for his introduction of solid-colored tableware (**Fiesta**™, **Harlequin, Riviera**), his impact on the white tableware produced by Homer Laughlin is equally important. Following **Virginia Rose** (1929), **Nautilus** (1935), and **Brittany** (1936), the Eggshell line of tableware was launched in 1937. Beginning with **Eggshell Nautilus** and **Eggshell Georgian**, it expanded to include **Swing** (1938) and **Theme** (designed to commemorate the World's Fair in 1939.) The Eggshell shapes proved to be quite popular and were featured in great quantities in the Montgomery Ward catalogs of the late 1930's through the early 1950's. Sears also sold Eggshell, but seems not to have offered as wide a variety as Wards. The combination of Rhead's designs and the technical genius of Bleininger and Thiemecke was unstoppable and HLC grew to become a vast china manufacturing complex.

In 1942 Frederick Rhead died of cancer. In 1945, Don Schreckengost joined HLC as art director. His handiwork can be seen in the **Jubilee**, **Debutante**, **Rhythm** and **Cavalier** shapes, which reflected a departure from the traditional lines to the more contemporary look. These shapes (among others) were to be the backbone of HLC production into the post-war years, when HLC became the largest pottery in the world. Although Mr. Schreckengost left HLC in 1960, he is still quite active in the pottery business today, working as a free-lance designer and supplying designs to several other potteries.

The company achieved outstanding success at providing china for the American home market for three quarters of a century. After World War II, china of increasingly lower prices began to be imported in quantity from other countries, notably Japan. Beginning in 1959, Homer Laughlin wisely diversified into hotel and restaurant china, and in the 1970's this product area surpassed that of china for home use. Today, the Homer Laughlin China Company is very much alive and well, being the largest manufacturer of china in the country. In addition to the copious output of institutional china, the factory today also again makes the highly-prized **Fiesta**™ in its classic shapes but in the new contemporary colors.

My visits to the Homer Laughlin plant have left me with a deep sense of this rich history. Due to a combination of low land prices and the particular nature of potteries, it is less costly to simply build a new factory than to upgrade an old one based on an obsolete manufacturing technology. As a result, there are many areas of the plant that have been shut down for years, yet which are completely unchanged from the last day of operation. I saw a tunnel kiln in which there were still carts filled with incompletely-fired china. (I think it was **Fiesta**™.) There are decorating rooms in which the decals were applied by scores of workers. Mr. Bob Jones, who presently works in the art department at HLC, began his career at HLC as a ware boy who moved the china to and from the decorators. He says he can still hear the calls for "ware boy!" when walking through some of these empty rooms.

Below I have listed some of the significant events that took place at the Homer Laughlin China Company from its beginning to the present. The primary purpose of this list is to show the time periods during which the various china shapes were produced. Unfortunately, it is much easier to mark the date when a shape began then when it ended. For some of the earlier shapes, the dates are uncertain, and are based on when a shape was advertised for sale. In other words, I have seen evidence that the shape in question was available at the time I have shown, but the shape *may* have been produced prior to that time and I have just not come across any evidence of the fact.

Homer Laughlin Historical Events

1871   Homer and Shakespeare Laughlin started their first pottery (2 kilns) in East Liverpool, Ohio.

1872   Laughlin Brothers received the $5,000.00 prize that was raised by the townspeople of East Liverpool as a reward to the first potter to produce white ware pottery.

1873   Construction of a plant on the west side of Harker Pottery. This was known as plant #1.

1877   Homer Laughlin purchased Shakespeare's business interest.

1884   China: Victor[1]

1896   China: Golden Gate (Homer Laughlin Combinets), Shakespeare@

1897   Homer Laughlin sold the factory and moved to Los Angeles. Louis I. Aaron took over as president with William E. Wells as general manager.

1899   Plant #2 was built at the East End section of East Liverpool.
         China: American Beauty

1901   Plant #3 was built along side Plant #2.
         China: Colonial, Seneca, Niagara

1903   China: King Charles

1907   Plant #4 began operations in Newell, West Virginia.
         China: Angelus, Empress
1911   Marcus Aaron took over as president succeeding his father, Louis I. Aaron.

1912   China: Hudson, Genesee

1914   Plant #5 was built just north of Plant #4.
         China: Majestic

1920	Dr. Albert Victor Bleininger, a noted ceramic engineer, joined the company to begin an era of major change in the art of china-making at HLC. China: Republic, Kwaker
1921	Construction of a lavish showroom so that customers could now be invited to come to the Homer Laughlin plant to view wares for sale. This display room of dark wood paneled walls and ceiling was made by Homer Laughlin pottery artists and was called "The Bower of Delights." This room is still in use today.
1923	Plant #6 was built, which included the first tunnel kiln.
1926	China: Yellowstone
1927	Frederick Hurten Rhead joined Homer Laughlin as head art designer. Between the two giants, Rhead and Bleininger, HLC would see a great outpouring of new designs and glazes.
1929	Plant #8 was built. This plant was subsequently devoted to the production of Virginia Rose and Marigold. China: Liberty
1931	W.E. Wells died and J.M. Wells became general manager.
1930-33	China: Wells, Century, Jade, Ravenna, Virginia Rose, Marigold, Nautilus (Regular) and Georgian/Craftsman.
1934	Harry Thiemecke joins HLC as a chemist.
1935	China: Fiesta™, Coronet
1936	China: Brittany, Harlequin
1937	China: Eggshell Nautilus, Eggshell Georgian
1938	First automated forming equipment introduced. China: Swing, Carnival, Riveria, Tango
1939	China: Theme, Kitchen Kraft, Serenade
1940	Marcus Lester Aaron became president. China: Picadilly
1942	Frederick Rhead died.
1945	Don Schreckengost joined HLC as art director.
1946	Dr. Bleininger died.

1948	Homer Laughlin's peak production year – over 10 million dozen. China: Jubilee, Skytone, Suntone and Debutante, Kraft Blue, Kraft Pink
1949-59	China: Rhythm, Cavalier, Triumph, Kenilworth, Epicure
1959	Hotel and restaurant china introduced.
1960	J.M. Wells Jr. became general manager.
1962	Vincent Broomhall joined HLC as art director.
1970	Hotel and institutional china production surpassed china sold to public.
1972	Harry Thiemecke retired. Dennis M. Newbury became art director, Jon D. Bentley became general superintendent.
1984	Jonathan O. Parry became art director.
1985	First fast fired kiln put in service.
1986	Fiesta™ reintroduced as a lead-free china product. J.M. Wells III became general manager.
1989	M.L. Aaron retires after 65 years of service. Marcus Aaron II became president.

Problems In Identifying Homer Laughlin China

Issues that inevitably face the collector of antique china include the positive identification of the piece or set, and the assignment of the china to a particular place in the history of the producer and the culture in which the china was used. Had the Homer Laughlin Company but foreseen years ago that antique collectors would be asking all sorts of difficult questions about the names of shapes and patterns, they might have obliged us by keeping detailed records of their every creation. The sad truth is that the china which is the subject of this book was produced to be used on a daily basis by ordinary people, rather than to be collected by antique hunters. It was sold through large mail-order firms and department stores. It was distributed as premiums to reward the purchaser of soaps, breakfast foods, and other household products. It was given away or sold in conjunction with coupon programs by grocery stores. The path from factory to user is often clouded and difficult to reconstruct.

China is identified by its shape or design and by the pattern or decorative treatment applied to each piece after its initial firing. While the shapes were given names by the company, and these names were subsequently used by the retailers or eventual suppliers of the china, the same cannot be said for the patterns. Obtaining the names for the different shapes of Homer Laughlin china has been rather easy compared to the naming of the decorative patterns. The Homer Laughlin Company proudly named each different shape which it produced. Names were assigned using a high degree of artistic freedom. Sometimes the names were commemorative, other times the names were intended to be descriptive of the feeling of the shape, and for still others there appears to be no rationale for the choice of a shape name. Nevertheless, the number of shapes is rather limited compared to the number of patterns used to decorate those shapes. Determining the name of an old HLC shape today is generally not a problem.

Pattern names were assigned in some cases by Homer Laughlin, and in other cases by the companies which sold the china to the public. There are even cases in which the same basic pattern was sold under different names by different distributors. In the early years of the twentieth century, it does not appear that either the factory or the major retailers such as Sears paid much attention to the formal naming of patterns. In looking through the Sears catalog pages from the early decades of the present century, there are many sets of Homer Laughlin china offered. The catalog provides what are certainly descriptive names (especially important since the catalog was not published in color.) Typical names found in the 1919-1920 period include: "Pink Rose Border and Gold Edge," "Violet Spray Gold Trimmed," and "Carnation Beauty Gold Ornamented." It is interesting to note that during this time period, the dinnerware in the Sears catalog was attributed to the "famous" Homer Laughlin China Company. For china made during this time, there are no specific names for the patterns for the simple reason that no one back then ever saw fit to give them names.

Later on, there was a general change in the approach to china marketing, both by the Homer Laughlin Company and by the retailers who sold Homer Laughlin China. There was a trend within companies such as Sears toward the use of house brand names, and toward the exclusion of any mention of the actual manufacturer of the china. At the same time, we see a rise of the use of "proper" names to identify the china decorations. All of the Eggshell ware certainly fall into this period.

China sold by mail-order through companies like Wards and Sears is much easier to associate with pattern names than is china sold over-the-counter by companies like Woolworth's. Woolworth's does not appear to have kept any records of the names of old china that they sold. Certainly I could find no one at that company that had any knowledge of, nor interest in, the subject. Thus many of the Virginia Rose patterns that were sold extensively by Woolworth's remain unnamed in the pages of this book. In some cases, names have been found within the archives of the Homer Laughlin Company. Where these were found, I have provided them in this book.

For cases where the pattern name is not known, I have resorted to the use of pattern numbers. The Homer Laughlin Company used pattern numbers for internal identification of decorations. These numbers consisted of 1-3 letters followed by 1-5 digits, which would uniquely identify both the shape (via the letters) and the decoration (the numbers) an example of this is Y306 on Yellowstone. However, sometimes the letters identify not the shape at all, but rather the large distributor for whom the pattern was destined. For example, W450 or JJ90 as used for Woolworth's and J.J. Newberry's respectively. Unfortunately for the collector, these identifications usually appear only on the bottoms of the serving bowls (although some have been found in other locations such as the inside of the casserole lids.) If a serving bowl can be found which bears such a number, then the pattern can be uniquely identified. If only a single plate or saucer is to be had, then the pattern identification may still remain a mystery. To further confuse the unfortunate collector, the same decal was sometimes used on different shapes. In this case, the pattern would carry an entirely different number on each of the shapes. Shown in Plate #1 are several different shapes, each having the "Colonial Kitchen" pattern. However, the pattern will have an entirely different number when it is associated with each of the shapes.

In the event this is not sufficiently confusing, there is also the matter of decal numbers. These numbers were assigned by the decal manufacturer, not HLC. Where I have used these numbers, I have clearly identified them as Decal Number such and such, not to be confused with the numbers which HLC assigned to the pattern themselves.

Plate 1

In the case of china pictured in this book for which even HLC pattern or decal numbers could not be established, I have chosen to provide temporary pattern identification which consists of 4 letters (to identify the shape) and 1-3 digits to identify the pattern. To my knowledge, HLC never used any more than three letters in a pattern identification, so this system will make my own temporary identifiers immediately obvious. To further set these apart as not being "official" HLC pattern designations, mine always are preceded by the letters: TEMP.

In addition to the problems of shape and pattern, there is the issue of which pieces were sold together. What pieces went into a set of a particular shape? The answer varies depending on the period in which the set was produced. In the early years of this century there was a much greater variety of pieces than in later times when dining became much simpler. A total of over 83 different pieces are offered in the Empress shape dating from around 1900, including an oyster tureen, a bone dish, a spoon holder, and a ramekin and stand. By the time of the **Eggshell** shapes in the late 1930's the typical set of pieces had been reduced to around 34. While this change was occuring, the names by which the different pieces were known also underwent a change from English names to American names. English Nappies became "round vegetable bowls," and English Bakers became "oval vegetable bowls." The naming and sizing guide on page 178 provides a more extensive cross-reference between trade names and common names of the various pieces.

The processes which allowed this interesting china to find its way into our hands today did not act equally on all pieces. For the older shapes, the platters are quite common. The serving dishes such as the casserole are also frequently found. On the other hand, cups and saucers from these older shapes are almost nonexistent. It is obvious that the china used on a daily basis fell victim to breakage far more often than did the platters, which were probably used only for special occasions. It has been my experience that the opposite is true for the more recent shapes, where we find the plates and everyday table service more often than the platters and serving dishes. I have no idea why this may be true. My husband thinks it may be because the serving dishes are still in use, while the everyday dishes have been discarded as old-fashioned, thus, finding their way into the antique markets.

A final problem with shapes and sets is the fact that the hollowware and flatware pieces of a set were not always unique to a particular shape. Thus, we have the case where the **Empress** and **Kwaker** shapes both share the same flatware. What probably happened, in this case, was that when the **Kwaker** shape was produced, it was decided to make only the hollowware, and to simply package this hollowware with the flatware from the earlier **Empress** shape. The practice of using salt and pepper shakers and butter dishes from one shape to fill out sets in another shape was widespread.

In the 1950's we find a tendency to mix and match hollowware and flatware for somewhat different reasons. Rather than just simplifying the manufacturing and distribution process by the sharing of a particular flatware or hollowware between two different shapes, we now find a tendency to make up sets from pieces taken from a much wider variety of shapes. At least two reasons for this approach can be identified. In some cases HLC found that the desired decorating schemes, particularly those involving solid colors, worked much better with certain hollowware piece shapes. **Charm House** hollowware was especially chosen for this role. In other cases it appears that the desires of the distributor of particular sets dictated what went into them. No other explanation can be found for a set like **Lady Stratford** and **Lady Greenbrier** patterns, which are made up of regular **Nautilus** (not **Eggshell**) flatware, two different types of hollowware (ordinary **Rhythm** and **Charm House**), and an **Eggshell Nautilus** teapot! The only common thread through this whole set is the decorative pattern.

Plate 2

when only the finest in

22 KARAT GOLD

will do

Exquisite, excitingly lovely! Never before have these authentic, luxurious royal patterns been offered by the famous old-world craftsmen of Homer Laughlin at a price so very, very low. Yes, each lovely piece is FIRST SELECTION . . . lavishly designed in 22K GOLD. Yes, they are beautiful . . . comparable to only the costliest of English China. You will want a set.

THE *Lady Stratford*   THE *Lady Greenbrier*

55 Pc. Service for 8 $39⁹⁵
100 Pc. Service for 12 $59⁹⁵

HOMER LAUGHLIN

WARRANTED 22 KT. GOLD

Lady Stratford *and* **Lady Greenbrier**. *This picture appeared in a brochure from Albert E. Sloan, Inc., which I obtained from Mr. Ed Carson of HLC. The flatware is regular Nautilus shape. The creamer, sugar, and casserole are Charm House shape. The sauce boat is Rhythm.*

Plate 3

These teapots were offered as "promotional" gifts and are **Eggshell Nautilus**. The unusual backstamp employed by A.E. Sloan is shown in the lower right of the illustration. Photographs of these dishes are shown on page 81.

Empress and Kwaker

Empress and Kwaker are described together because, while their hollowwares were significantly different, they shared the same flatware. Empress and Kwaker are definitely "old" styles. Lois Lehner states that the Empress mark is found in china from around 1900. Abundant offerings of Empress can be found in Sears Roebuck catalogs from as early as 1919. Butler Brothers shows Kwaker in their 1925 catalog. Although they were marketed into the 1940's, they make no attempt to conceal their ties to the early years of the twentieth century.

From examples consisting of both actual pieces and catalog advertisements, it appears that both Empress and Kwaker decorations tended toward narrow and ornate bands on an otherwise plain background, medallions, and gold and white treatments. Kwaker appears to have made a significant use of floral decorations, while I have never seen Empress with these. Empress shows evidence of its earlier origins in its larger variety of pieces. The Homer Laughlin catalog for the period identifies eighty-three different pieces, including individual cream, sugar, and butter dishes, and bone dishes, which are not found in later sets. In contrast, Kwaker lists only sixty-five different pieces.

Empress and Kwaker hollowware pieces are immediately distinguishable from one another by means of the shapes of their handles. The Empress handle is almost ear-shaped, and displays no flat segments. On the other hand, Kwaker handles invariably have a flat top which meets the downward-sweeping segment in a sharp angle. The Kwaker handle is reminiscent of the handle that one might find on a lamp from which a genie would emerge.

The body shapes of the two hollowware pieces are also quite different. The lower portion of the Empress body will curve outward to an obvious ridge about one third of the way up from the bottom. The upper two thirds will slope inward to an obvious ridge or lip. Kwaker, on the other hand, shows a clear bowl shape for perhaps three-fourths of the way to the top of the piece, then turns sharply inward to the opening or lid. The differences in the shapes, and especially in the handles, are immediately obvious. The unique shapes of the handles makes it possible to recognize Empress and Kwaker hollowware pieces from a distance when combing antique china shops.

The flatware of Empress and Kwaker also bears uniquely distinguishing characteristics. Platters, which are frequently found in antique shops, are easily recognized by the following characteristics:

- *The verge drops steeply down from the rim to the well. This characteristic can be easily felt when the piece is handled.*

- *The rim at the ends of the platter is wider than the rim at the sides of the piece. This difference in rim width is so obvious that it is even apparent in the rather primitive artwork of the early Sears catalogs.*

- *The narrow but ornate border on the otherwise white background will always catch the eye when the piece is mingled with others on the shelves of the antique dealers.*

Plate 4

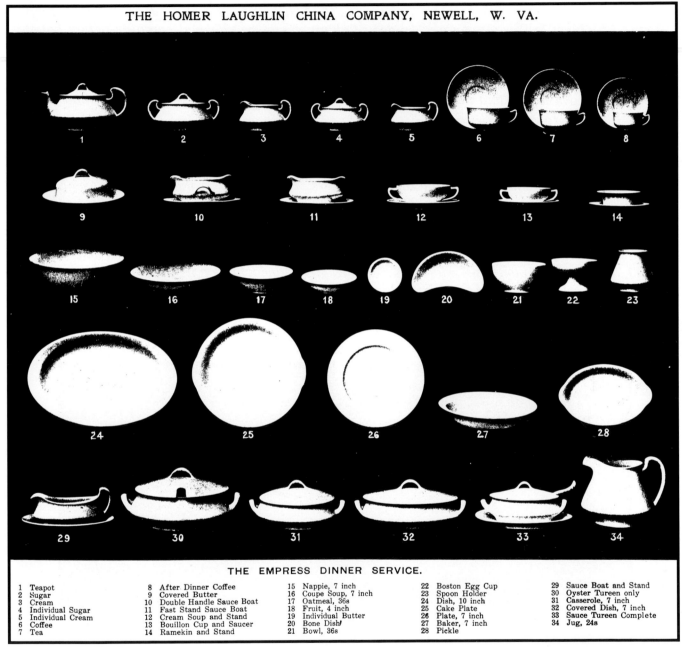

THE HOMER LAUGHLIN CHINA COMPANY, NEWELL, W. VA.

THE EMPRESS DINNER SERVICE.

1 Teapot	8 After Dinner Coffee	15 Nappie, 7 inch	22 Boston Egg Cup	29 Sauce Boat and Stand
2 Sugar	9 Covered Butter	16 Coupe Soup, 7 inch	23 Spoon Holder	30 Oyster Tureen only
3 Cream	10 Double Handle Sauce Boat	17 Oatmeal, 36s	24 Dish, 10 inch	31 Casserole, 7 inch
4 Individual Sugar	11 Fast Stand Sauce Boat	18 Fruit, 4 inch	25 Cake Plate	32 Covered Dish, 7 inch
5 Individual Cream	12 Cream Soup and Stand	19 Individual Butter	26 Plate, 7 inch	33 Sauce Tureen Complete
6 Coffee	13 Bouillon Cup and Saucer	20 Bone Dish	27 Baker, 7 inch	34 Jug, 24s
7 Tea	14 Ramekin and Stand	21 Bowl, 36s	28 Pickle	

This page from the 1927 HLC catalog shows some of the pieces available in Empress.

*Plate 5: Covered casserole with "Empress" on backstamp. On the underside of the lid is "GB," standing for **Gold Band**. In the Sears catalog of 1920, this pattern is called **Colonial Gold Band**. In 1927 Sears called it **Bright Gold Band**. Butler Brothers (1925) called it **Capitol**.*

*Plate 6: An unidentified Empress pattern **TEMP EMPR 102**. This regal pattern provided me with an object lesson in why each piece of china should be checked carefully before being purchased. I picked these pieces up at a swap meet, and found when I got it home that some of the fruits and the plates were Bavarian china, and not HLC at all. The patterns were so similar that a careful comparison was required to distinguish between the two types of china. In this case, the backstamps told the tale. Shown: Cake Plate, 9" Dish (platter), 10" plate, and fruits (the real HLC.)*

*Plate 7: An assortment of patterns on Empress. The pattern on the coupe soup is called **Bowknot**. It is a simple design consisting of gold bows and a gold line on the rim, with a second line in purple ⅛" below the gold. The larger of the two platters, the 17" dish (platter) shown (whose pattern I have designated as **TEMP EMPR 103**) has a single band of small pink roses and orange flowers on a pale blue background. The 15" dish (platter), designated **TEMP EMPR 123**, has a band of pink roses with leaves of blue, green, and white on a gold background.*

Plate 5

*The creamer in this picture was called **Yellow Matte Gold Band** in the 1927 Sears catalog. The gold on the creamer is a matte gold, while the gold on the casserole is bright.*

Plate 6

Plate 7

*Plate 8: Pattern **HLC #E4613** on the Empress 8" dish (platter.) This elaborate and very elegant decal is centered on each of the two long sides of the dish. It consists of birds with outspread wings on either side of a vase filled with flowers. It has a gold edge and a gold line around each end of the verge, connecting the two patterns on the sides. This same decal can be found on Yellowstone in the 1939 Sears catalog, where it is called Caledonia, and on Kwaker (with HLC decal number of 9504.)*

Plate 9: Pattern TEMP EMPR 105 on a 9" dish (platter) and a pickle. This decoration is similar in layout to E4613 shown in Plate #8. It consists of two large decals on each of the long sides of the dish. Each decal shows a cobalt blue medallion with a vase holding two orange roses and a white flower in the center. There is a gold edge and a second gold line below connecting the two decals.

*Plate 10: Two 10" Empress plates. Left: **Rose and Lattice** pattern. The name comes from the Sears catalog of 1927. It has a tan lattice border with panels of small pink roses which alternate with large pink roses in a medallion. Right: **TEMP EMPR 106**. Dark green medallion with pink rose and blue ribbon in the middle.*

Plate 8

Plate 9

Plate 10

Plate 11

Plate 12

Plate 13

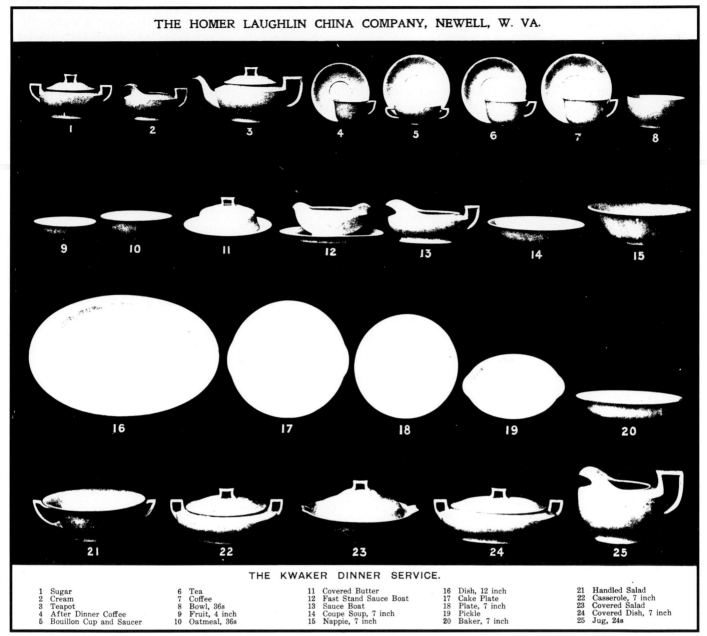

THE HOMER LAUGHLIN CHINA COMPANY, NEWELL, W. VA.

THE KWAKER DINNER SERVICE.

1	Sugar	6	Tea	11	Covered Butter	16 Dish, 12 inch	21 Handled Salad
2	Cream	7	Coffee	12	Fast Stand Sauce Boat	17 Cake Plate	22 Casserole, 7 inch
3	Teapot	8	Bowl, 36s	13	Sauce Boat	18 Plate, 7 inch	23 Covered Salad
4	After Dinner Coffee	9	Fruit, 4 inch	14	Coupe Soup, 7 inch	19 Pickle	24 Covered Dish, 7 inch
5	Bouillon Cup and Saucer	10	Oatmeal, 36s	15	Nappie, 7 inch	20 Baker, 7 inch	25 Jug, 24s

*Plate 11: The plate on the right shows **HLC Decal Number 6115**. It consists of a black border containing tiny roses with another border of groups of larger pink roses on a yellow background. There is a gold line around the verge. The plate on the left is decorated with **HLC #W530**. Groups of roses enclose green sections, each of which contain a medallion with roses in the center. There is a gold line around the verge.*

Plate 12: Pattern TEMP EK108. The only way to tell the difference between a piece of Empress and Kwaker flatware is by identification of the pattern. The same blanks were used for both and I don't know if this is Empress or Kwaker. The decals appear to be the same as the one shown on a Yellowstone pattern called Raymond, which appears in Jo Cunningham's book[4].

Plate 13: This page from the 1927 HLC catalog shows some of the pieces available in Kwaker.

*Plate 14: Pattern **HLC #W226**, the "W" in the pattern number indicates it was a Woolworth's pattern. This decoration consists of a gold band in a grape leaf motif around the edge of the lid, around the top of the piece adjacent to the lid, and a small strip of the same pattern on top of each of the handles. Along with these bands are three decals on the lid, and two on the body, consisting of yellow roses and yellow flowers in a vine motif done in black. On the piece pictured here, the placement of the flower decals is not uniform. Also of note is the fact that the same gold ivy band is used on the pieces shown in Plate 15. The flower decals were individually applied by hand. The off-center placement of the flower decal on the pieces shown is no doubt due to the combination of manual application and the high production rates of the HLC plant.*

Plate 15: Pattern TEMP KWAK 110. This covered dish, which belonged to my grandmother, was the start of my love affair with Homer Laughlin china. My first attempt to identify it led me to believe it was a Virginia Rose gravyboat. I look back at this mistake today and laugh. Its white body sets off decals of full roses of red and yellow. Both the body and lid have a ring of a gold stamped design. My husband came home with the exact duplicate of this dish, which I sent to a friend who lives in Rome, Italy. Also shown is a casserole in this pattern. I discovered not one but two in an antique store out in the California desert area. This leads me to believe that this was a popular pattern.

*Plate 16: Pattern **HLC #K8904B**. This set is perhaps my favorite. Since I don't know the HLC name for this pattern, I have taken to calling it "Nasturtium" for very obvious reasons. The Nasturtiums that dot the white body of this china are a vivid orange, yellow, and green. The handles are heavily edged in gold. Shown are: 15" dish (platter), casserole, covered dish, sauce boat, and creamer.*

Plate 14

Plate 15

Plate 16

Plate 17: Right: **Neville**, *Pattern* **HLC #2253** *on a Kwaker coupe soup. This pattern, according to HLC records, was made exclusively for Sears. The Neville name appears in the Sears catalogs all during the 1940's. Sears describes the patterns "tiny pink rosebuds nestled in tan scrolls which are part of the narrow green and black border." HLC describes the pattern "4 sprigs, gold verge." On the left is an 11" dish (platter) decorated in a pattern that is identical to Neville except for the color scheme. If the HLC pattern number is ever located, it will probably be close to 2253. Meanwhile, I will identify it as TEMP KWAK 112.*

Plate 18: Pattern **HLC #K3415M**. *This Kwaker casserole is banded with pale blue, with inserts of white on which appear pink roses and yellow flowers. The handles are decorated in burnished gold.*

Plate 19: Pattern **HLC #K3415M**. *A Kwaker 11" covered dish, banded with white flowers edged in blue and blue leaves edged in white, on a burnt orange background. The handles are covered in matte gold. The effect is one of great elegance, rather suggestive of a Greek antiquity. I think of these covered oval dishes as casseroles, but their tradename is "covered dish." The round covered serving dishes such as the one shown in Plate 18 are known to the trade as a "casserole."*

Plate 17

Plate 18

Plate 19

Plate 20: Pattern **HLC #K8677**. *The pattern has a band of alternate groups of apples and grapes, each group of fruit surrounded by a decorative blue border, with small tan shapes between each group of fruit. This same pattern, which Sears called "Fruit Decorated Ivory Body" can be seen on Yellowstone in the 1928 catalog. Shown is the 17" dish (platter) and the baker.*

Plate 21: **HLC #K9177M** *is the pattern for this 15" dish (platter). The pattern consists of a band of roses, with a solid tan between the roses and the edge of the piece. The pattern on the 9" baker is* **HLC #K3577M**. *It consists of groups of roses and blue flowers on a yellow background, separated by medallions. There is a thin gold line around the verge. Note the one section of the decoration (at about 11o'clock) around the rim which is longer than the others. It would appear that the decal came in a continuous strip, and that the pattern simply did not fit around the piece an exact number of times. The same effect can be seen on the baker in Plate 20.*

Plate 22: **Darcy**, *Pattern* **HLC #K8124**. *This pattern which is shown in the 1941 Sears Roebuck catalog has the backstamp "Darcy" in gold along with the Homer Laughlin logo. This pattern is also seen on Eggshell Georgian as "Countess." Shown are: 13" dish (platter), 10" plate, and 9" baker.*

Plate 20

Plate 21

Plate 22

The Republic shape dates back to the early days of Homer Laughlin Company. Its production started in the early 1900's, and lasted well into the 1940's. We find in an advertisement in the Sears catalog from 1919-1920 that a set of Republic billed as a "Violet Spray Gold Trimmed Dinner Set," all 112 pieces, could be had for $23.98. Two decades later, in 1941, we have another Sears catalog entry for a pattern called "Calais" in what is obviously Republic. The ad states that this shape and pattern has been popular for generations, and that it is suggestive of the Victorian era. At this time, a 95-piece service for 12 could be had for the price of $17.95. I have a beautiful sugar bowl in the Republic shape (Plate 25) whose back stamp indicates it was made in 1945. I also have a set of Republic which bears a date of 1947.

The Republic shape, according to an HLC catalog, was available in a total of over 65 different pieces, including a bone dish, and individual cream, sugar, and butter dish. Clearly the shape was designed to fit a much earlier style of elegant dining.

All of the pieces making up the Republic shape are quite ornately styled. Generally, the plates and bowls are characterized by a scalloped edge with a repeated embossed pattern (see Plate 24) somewhat like Virginia Rose which followed much later. The hollowware pieces all have a distinctive shape which almost gives the impression that the pieces were made in two parts, a top half and a bottom half, which were then attached to make the finished piece. The bottom portion of the piece slopes outward to a definite sharp ridge, from which the sides then slope straight inward to the top of the piece. The handles of the various serving pieces are relatively large. They have a ruffled feel, with a decided upward sweep. The handles on the lids are in the form of a flattened open loop.

The decorations used with Republic were, for the most part, floral designs. Pieces were usually trimmed in gold. While most of the designs were lightly colored decals, I have also found designs which consist only of the outlines of flowers, done in gold (see Plate 27.)

Today, Republic is somewhat hard to find. Most of mine were found in a second-hand shop in Palmdale, California, out in the Mojave desert near Los Angeles. Still, a careful scrutiny of antique shops which carry American china can yield pleasant surprises.

Plate 23 is a page from an HLC catalog, dating from 1927, which shows some of the many pieces available in the Republic shape. A complete list of all of the pieces available in this shape is contained in the value guide. Note, however, that this pictures older pieces such as the bone dish, and the individual butter, cream, and sugar. Watch as these progressively disappear from the newer shapes, reflecting the changes in dining habits and customer preferences.

Plate 23

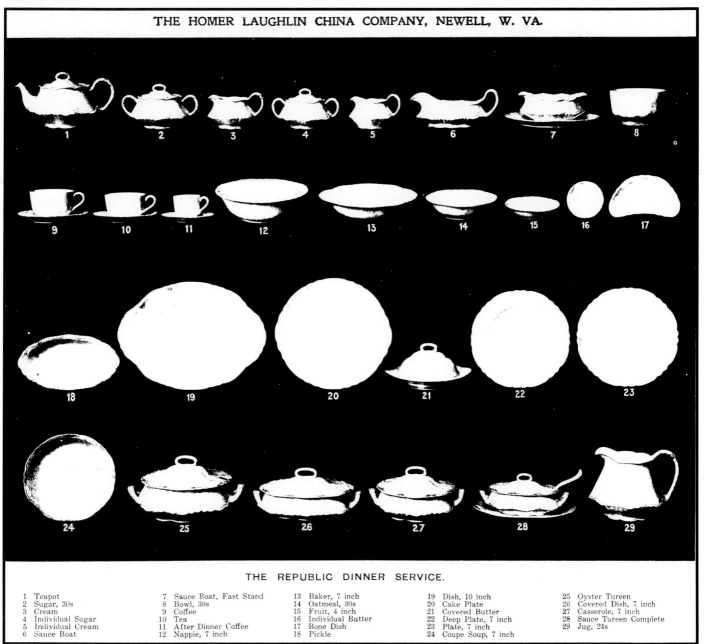

THE HOMER LAUGHLIN CHINA COMPANY, NEWELL, W. VA.

THE REPUBLIC DINNER SERVICE.

1 Teapot	7 Sauce Boat, Fast Stand	13 Baker, 7 inch	19 Dish, 10 inch	25 Oyster Tureen
2 Sugar, 30s	8 Bowl, 30s	14 Oatmeal, 30s	20 Cake Plate	26 Covered Dish, 7 inch
3 Cream	9 Coffee	15 Fruit, 4 inch	21 Covered Butter	27 Casserole, 7 inch
4 Individual Sugar	10 Tea	16 Individual Butter	22 Deep Plate, 7 inch	28 Sauce Tureen Complete
5 Individual Cream	11 After Dinner Coffee	17 Bone Dish	23 Plate, 7 inch	29 Jug, 24s
6 Sauce Boat	12 Nappie, 7 inch	18 Pickle	24 Coupe Soup, 7 inch	

Plate 24

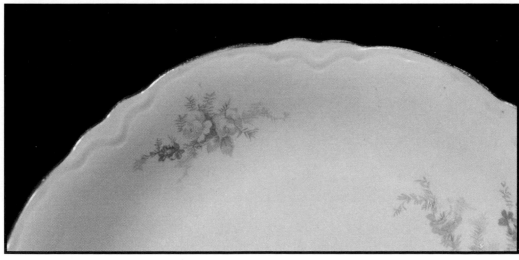

Plate 25: Rear: **Wayside**, Pattern **HLC #CP100**. This 7" plate with the Cunningham and Pickett backstamp is decorated with only a large decal of a pink rose, yellow and blue flowers, and a purple tulip. The "CP" in the pattern number indicates it was a special Cunningham and Pickett pattern.

Front: TEMP RPBL 132. A very attractive decoration consisting of a gold scroll with pink flowers and strawberries on a covered sugar bowl.

Plate 26: **Jean**. The trade journal China, Glass and Lamps dated November 1942 provided the name for this pattern. The pale purple, pink and white flower decal can also be found on other shapes. This pattern must have been sold in large quantities because it seems easier to find. Shown: coupe soup and sauce bowl.

Plate 27: **Golden Rose**. Darlene Nossaman gave me the name of this pattern. That name certainly seems to describe very well the gold stamps on the rims of this set. The same pattern can also be seen on Virginia Rose. Shown: 10" plate, 7" baker, 9" dish (platter), cup and saucer, and fruit.

Plate 25

Plate 26

Plate 27

The Yellowstone shape is one of several which were first produced during the 1920's. It dates from the period before Frederick Rhead joined the company, when outside designers were used to develop new shapes. Yellowstone was probably the last shape designed by this method, since Rhead joined Homer Laughlin in 1927 and shortly thereafter began to exercise his influence over subsequent artistic work.

Yellowstone was characterized by an octagonal theme which carried through virtually all of the pieces of this shape, and by a light yellow body over which an ivory glaze was applied. This glaze had a higher gloss than the vellum glaze that was later used with Century. It is somewhat amusing to read advertisements from the time when Yellowstone was first announced, in which HLC touted the fact that they had broken away from the "dead white" body of earlier designs. HLC was originally founded on the ability of Mr. Homer Laughlin to produce that same "dead white" china in contrast to the yellowish products of other potters in the area.

The Yellowstone shape was quite widely sold, at least in the beginning of its production run. In an advertisement in *The Pottery, Glass & Brass Salesman* from March 31, 1927, HLC informs us that approximately 40% of their entire plant capacity was, during the last half of 1926, devoted to the production of this shape. The production of Yellowstone during that period approached 10,000 dozens per day, all decorated. HLC further informs us that this quantity of china would stretch for 10 miles. We find it to be somewhat rare in antique shops today, certainly far more so than some of the Eggshell shapes discussed later in this volume. While looking through shops for the occasional pieces that might be found, one cannot help but marvel at the incredible amount of destruction which this beautiful shape incurred in the course of daily use. As a girl, I remember my grandmother's china. Her china for special occasions was Kwaker (of which I have one piece), but her everyday china was Yellowstone. I have several pieces of this which appear later in these pages.

The most noteworthy characteristics of Yellowstone, as mentioned above, is its octagonal shape and its ivory glaze. The octagonal shape is most evident in the hollowware such as the casserole and the cream and sugar. While the flatware continues the eight-sided theme, it is more subdued. The teacup has a round rim while the sides continue the faceted theme of the shape. The handles of the cream, sugar, and teacup are ear-shaped with a flattened top. The handles on the lids of the casserole and sugar are simple, flattened knobs. The foot of the hollowware is either diminished or lacking entirely. The overall impression of this shape, especially when looking at some of the patterns (such as Rosetta) is that Yellowstone properly belongs in the Arts and Crafts period which predated the china by 15-20 years.

Some of the pieces available in Yellowstone appear in the 1927 HLC catalog, Plate 28. The pictures shown do not encompass the full scope of Yellowstone, as can be seen by the complete list of pieces in the value guide. An examination of this list will reveal the fact that the bone dish is no more, but that the individual butter, cream, and sugar are still with us. Of all the pieces shown in the 1927 catalog, my absolute favorite is the jug.

Plate 28

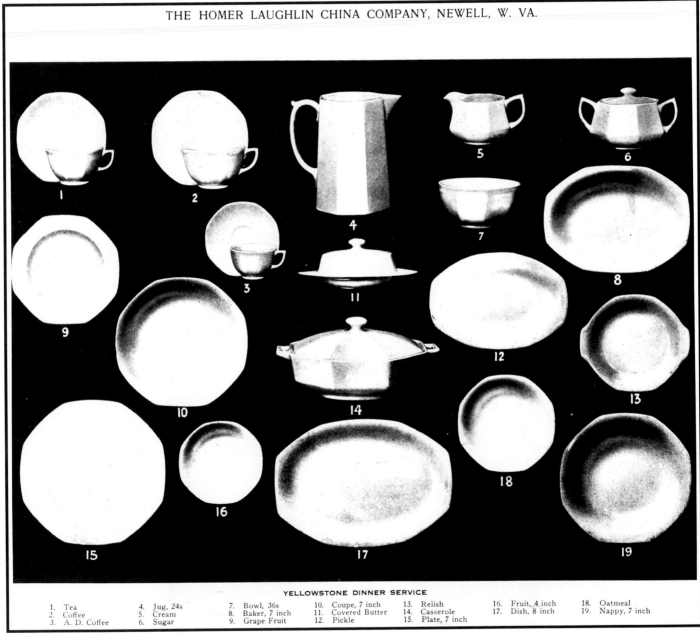

THE HOMER LAUGHLIN CHINA COMPANY, NEWELL, W. VA.

YELLOWSTONE DINNER SERVICE

1. Tea	4. Jug, 24s	7. Bowl, 36s	10. Coupe, 7 inch	13. Reiish	16. Fruit, 4 inch	18. Oatmeal
2. Coffee	5. Cream	8. Baker, 7 inch	11. Covered Butter	14. Casserole	17. Dish, 8 inch	19. Nappy, 7 inch
3. A. D. Coffee	6. Sugar	9. Grape Fruit	12. Pickle	15. Plate, 7 inch		

This page from the HLC 1927 catalog shows some of the pieces avaliable in Yellowstone.

Plate 29: **Golden Rose**. *On an ivory body are yellow flowers and black leaves. The pieces are outlined in black. This pattern is named and shown in the 1927 Sears Roebuck catalog. Personally I don't think the flowers look at all like roses but it is positively named Golden Rose. Shown is a 7" coupe soup.*

Plate 30: Pattern **HLC #W127/30**. *This pattern was on the Yellowstone china used by my grandmother for everyday meals. For a while I confused it with the pattern called Raymond seen in Jo Cunningham's book[5] but have since come to realize that it is not the same. Of course, I'm working hard to track down a name since it is of special interest to me. I was glad to find the Homer Laughlin number on several plates at the factory. Because it starts with a 'W", my grandmother may have bought it in the local Woolworth's. Shown: 13" dish (platter), butter dish, cream, and sugar. (Photographed by Norman Nossaman, from the collection of Darlene Nossaman.)*

Plate 31: Pattern **HLC #Y795**. *Another of the many unknown HLC pattern names. The highlight of this set is the deep bowl and the relish which shows wide, slightly indented, handles. The flowers and leaves are highly stylized and have a definite Art Deco look. Against a white body the orange flowers and black, yellow, and gray leaves are outstanding. Shown are deep 5" bowl, 9" plate, relish, cup and saucer, and teapot.*

Plate 29

Plate 30

Plate 31

Plate 32: **Wild Rose**. *Pattern* **HLC #Y220**. *I found this set at the large swap meet which is held at the Rose Bowl in Pasadena, CA each month. It has a sugar bowl that is larger than any I have come across. The name "Wild Rose" comes from the Huxford's Fiesta™ book⁶. shown are: casserole, creamer, and large sugar.*

Plate 33: **Pink Moss Rose**. *This pattern can be found in the 1927 Sears Roebuck catalog, where it is described as consisting "of a cluster of pink moss roses with delicate autumn foliage. Extending from each side of the cluster is a delicate pea green line which encircles each piece." Shown: 14" dish (platter.)*

Plate 34: Pattern **HLC #W132**. *This decal of very subdued yellow-orange roses blends well under the warm ivory glaze. The roses look quite realistic. 14" dish (platter) and 6" plate.*

Plate 32

Plate 33

Plate 34

Plate 35: **Rosetta**. *This pattern, which displays an exotic bird of red, green, yellow, and black above a spray of flowers in various tones of orange and yellow was a very exciting find. This is another set that I wanted to own ever since I saw it in Jo Cunningham's book[7]. I believe the black lines do a good job of emphasizing the angular motif of the Yellowstone sauce boat.*

Plate 36: A page from April 26, 1928, The Pottery, Glass, and Brass Salesman, *a trade magazine. This page is interesting for a variety of reasons. For one thing, it associates HLC pattern **Y21** with a specific decal. Although the colors of the pieces are not apparent, the decal could still be easily recognized. Second, at the bottom of the page we can see a list of the shapes being advertised by HLC in the Spring of 1928. We can see here on the one hand, that the older shapes "Empress" and "Hudson" (which began production around the turn of the century) are still being sold. At the same time we can see "Newell," the first shape designed by Frederick Rhead, is available the very next year after he joined the company. Finally, note the lettering at the bottom of the picture of the china, which is quite suggestive of an even earlier period than that of the advertisement itself.*

Plate 35

Opposite Page
Plate 36

The
Homer Laughlin China Company
Presents

THE YELLOWSTONE

Decoration: Y.21

A RECORD FOR CONTINUOUS PRODUCTION AND INCREASING DEMAND ARE CONVINCING EVIDENCE OF THE RETAIL POWER OF THE YELLOWSTONE DINNER SERVICE . . . THE GRACEFUL AND INTERESTING SHAPE, THE CAREFULLY SELECTED PATTERNS, AND SCIENTIFIC POTTING ARE FACTORS WHICH HAVE CONTRIBUTED TO THIS UNPRECEDENTED SUCCESS.

LAUGHLIN SHAPES

THE HUDSON	THE EMPRESS	THE YELLOWSTONE
THE REPUBLIC	THE KWAKER	THE NEWELL

The
Homer Laughlin China Company, Newell, W. Va.
SEVEN FACTORIES: EAST LIVERPOOL, OHIO, and NEWELL, W. VA.

Plate 37: Pattern TEMP YELL 148. This Yellowstone teapot should certainly have been named "Chrysanthemum," since it features a large pink and yellow chrysanthemum decal.

Plate 38: Pattern TEMP YELL 149. The 10" dish (platter) shows an interesting decoration consisting of three floral groups made up of red, pink, and yellow flowers. An exotic bird can be seen amongst the flowers of one of the groups. The AD cup and saucer is decorated with an unidentified pattern I have designated TEMP YELL 159. I have seen this pattern used on other shapes when I visited the HLC plant, but I have yet to get a positive identification of it as used on Yellowstone. Appearing on Newell, it is known as HLC #N3628.

Plate 39: Left: **Caledonian***, on the 9" plate. This pattern is shown in the 1929 Sears Roebuck catalog, where it was sold under the Sunrise Dinnerware brand name, a house trademark of Sears at that time. This brand name was also used by Sears with the Empress and Newell shapes. The decal consists of birds on either side of an urn of flowers. This decal also appears on the Empress shown in Plate 8. Right: Pattern TEMP YELL 150 on another 9" plate. It is interesting to note the differences between the plate on the left, with the white body, and the one on the right, with the ivory glaze. The dish on the right was in such mint condition that I could hardly believe the 1922 date in the backstamp.*

Plate 37

Plate 38

Plate 39

Started in 1927, Newell was the first shape designed by Frederick Rhead after joining Homer Laughlin. It did not appear to be a popular offering and was discontinued after a run of only 10 years or so. Newell appears to be a transitional shape, bridging between the highly ornate creations of the past (such as Republic) and the later, more simplified designs. The appearance of this bridge can be seen even better when Newell is compared with Liberty, which followed Newell in 1928. Although the flatware is similar, the hollowware is quite different, with the Liberty being free of the heavy embossing which characterized the Newell shape.

The Newell flatware has a gadroon edge (Plate 40), but this edge is less pronounced than on the later Liberty. The Newell plates have a definite scalloped edge. On Newell platters the scalloped effect is even more pronounced (Plate 44.) The cream continues the scalloped edge motif with the gadroon embossing appearing both on the edge and the foot. The gravy is essentially an elongated version of the cream. For both of these, the handles bear careful examination. These are not simple, functional attachments but instead form a part of the decorative scheme. On both the bottom and the top, the handles end in a sort of fan shape, which blends into the body. The top of the handle of the gravy boat is decorated with delicate scroll-work that blends with the gadroon embossing.

While Newell platters are regularly encountered, the same cannot be said for the other pieces which make up this shape. This is no doubt due both to the antiquity of the shape (now about 60 years old) and the short period of production. To further add to the difficulty of collecting Newell, some of the pieces (such as the sugar shown in Plate 41) do not look like "typical" HLC china, and are, thus, likely to be overlooked. Newell, especially the hollowware, should be regarded as a somewhat rare shape.

Plate 40

Plate 40: Details of Yellowstone edge.

Plate 41

Plate 41: This photo was provided by Mr. Ed Carson. It is probably from an old HLC catalog.

Newell Dinner Service

1. Coffee
2. Sugar
3. Casserole
4. Cream
5. Teacup & Saucer
6. Bowl, 36's, 1⅛ pint
7. Teapot
8. Sauce Boat
9. Ad Cup & Saucer
10. Nappy, 9"
11. Dish (Platter)

12. Pickle
13. Boullion Cup & Saucer
14. Cake Plate
15. Covered Butter
16. Plate, 9"
17. Coupe, 9"
18. Fruit, 5"
19. Fast Stand Sauce Boat
20. Jug, 24's, 4 pint
21. Sauce Boat and Pickle
22. Oatmeal, 36's, 5"

Plate 42

*Plate 42: Pattern **HLC #N2023**. This 9" baker was purchased at the huge Rose Bowl Swap Meet.*

Plate 43: (Facing Page). A Homer Laughlin advertisement from the February 2, 1928 issue of The Pottery, Glass, and Brass Salesman *which shows Newell with pattern **N 2023**. The same pattern can be seen above in Plate 42. It is very exciting to see the original ad when this pattern was new, and then see the actual dish that the ad describes. The ad also informs us that in 1928 HLC was offering five other shapes besides Newell.*

Opposite Page
Plate 43

Plate 44: Pattern TEMP NEWE 164. This old pattern of Victorian style flowers seems more fitting for a lady's boudoir than for dinner dishes. However, its delicate beauty makes me long to find other pieces. Shown: 13" dish (platter.)

*Plate 45: Left: Pattern **HLC #N3528**. This 9" nappy has a glossy yellow glaze with bright yellow and orange flowers in the decal. The color of the glaze is not uniform. When the dish is examined closely, it appears that the glaze flows when it is fired, and becomes thicker in the hollows than on the raised parts of the dish. The effect is actually quite pleasing, and reminds one of a hand-made dish. I have only seen this unusual glaze on Newell. I asked Mr. Thiemecke if he knew anything about it, but it evidently predated his tenure at HLC. The coupe soup on the right features the **Song of Spring** pattern. This pattern was sold by Sear Roebuck under the "Sunrise Dinnerware" label, and was pictured in the 1929 catalog. The decal is rather fanciful, in that it features roses, grapes, and plums all growing on the same large branch.*

Plate 46: Pattern TEMP NEWE 166. Like the nappy shown in Plate 45, this sauce boat and 11½" dish (platter) display bright, stylized flowers on a unique yellow glaze. The non-uniformity of the glaze is readily apparent.

Plate 44

Plate 45

Plate 46

The Liberty shape dates from the earliest years of Mr. Rhead's career at Homer Laughlin, having been brought out in 1928. Liberty was a slightly modified version of Newell, which was one of the less successful of the Homer Laughlin creations. The Liberty shape was produced into the 1950's. Liberty was sold mostly to high volume distributors, such as Albert E. Sloan and the C.G. Murphy Company.

The shape itself has elegant lines, especially some of the hollowware such as the casserole and the teapot. From a manufacturing standpoint Liberty was considered to be a good "potting" shape (i.e. it was easy to manufacture.) In spite of its simple lines, the Liberty shape can truly come into its own with the proper decoration. On the pages which follow, you will see the delightful transformation which can be brought about by a strong decorative pattern.

The Liberty shape is characterized by a "Gadroon" edge (Plate 47), which appears on all pieces. This edge consists of an embossing in the form of a delicate braid. It was usually highlighted in gold or platinum. The edges of the flatware have a slightly scalloped effect, which serves to break up the otherwise rather plain rim. The hollowware serving pieces are much more interesting, characterized by a pronounced foot. The lid handles have the form of flattened knobs on short posts. The handles on cups, cream and sugar, and the gravy boat are somewhat ear-shaped, with tops that are flattened and downward sloping toward the point of attachments. The handles of the casserole are simple loops.

*Plate 48: **Greenbriar**, Pattern **HLC CP96**. This pattern was named by Cunningham and Pickett whose backstamp it bears. It is not to be confused with the Eggshell Georgian Greenbriar, which is a completely different pattern, or with the Nautilus Lady Greenbrier which is both spelled differently and is also a different pattern, or with Theme shown in Plate 175, which uses the same decal, but which does not have the same name. Shown: 10" plate, 7" plate, sugar with lid, cream, and cup and saucer. (Photographed by Norman Nossaman, from the collection of Darlene Nossaman.)*

Plate 49: Left: Pattern TEMP LIBE 173. I picked up this unusual plate in East Liverpool, Ohio. The rim has a gold stamp that is quite unusual for Liberty. The center decal is also worthy of note. It shows what appears to be an oriental figure (a woman or young man) in some sort of pavilion in a forest setting. On the right is another unidentified pattern (TEMP LIBE 183) which appears on an 11½" dish (platter). The graceful pink poppies twined about green leaves create a very pleasing effect.

Plate 47

Plate 48

Plate 49

*Plate 50: The 7" baker on the right is **Apple Blossom, HLC #W246**. This pattern consists of pink apple blossoms with green leaves. The pattern has a hand-painted look to it. The "W" prefix to this pattern designation indicates it was sold by Woolworth's. I found this pattern on a piece at the HLC factory, with the pattern number on the back. I found the association with Woolworth's through a search of some old files in the HLC archives. The nappy on the left has a pattern identification of **HLC #L615**. The "L" prefix to the number indicates this is a "house" pattern of HLC, rather than one associated specifically with a certain customer. This pattern consists of pink, purple, and yellow daisies.*

Plate 51: Right: Pattern TEMP LIBR 175 on the 12" dish (platter). The pattern is made up of flowers in petit point, with an intricate gold stamp on the rim. Left: Pattern TEMP LIBR 185 on the 14" dish (platter). This pattern consists of a realistic apple blossom, with a gold stamp on the rim which are identical on both pieces.

*Plate 52: **Queen Esther**. The large rose decal was used on other shapes, but the unusual gold stamp, which is reminiscent of a crown, makes this pattern rather special. The unique pattern on the rim is echoed in the backstamp (Plate 53). Out of curiosity, I researched Queen Esther and found that she was the Jewish wife of the Persian King Xerxes, who saved her people from slaughter by Haman, a Persian official who sought the destruction of the Jews.*

Plate 50

Plate 51

Plate 52

Plate 53

Plate 54: **Lattice Rose**. *I was not surprised when a backstamp of 'Lattice Rose" was found on this set. This pattern has a background of a gray-white lattice on which are large dark pink roses, rosebuds and green rose leaves. Shown are: Plate 9" and Teapot.*

Plate 55: TEMP LIBE 180. My picture does not do justice to this pattern. It features one large white rose and very dark green rose leaves. Shown are: a deep plate (rimmed soup) and 7" plates.

Plate 56: **Sun Gold** *is the name of this pattern. I found this casserole, with the Currier and Ives decals, on the back shelf of an old, funky antique store called Rhoda's Place in the San Fernando Valley near Los Angeles. It was covered with so much dirt and dust that my husband, who also is an avid Homer Laughlin finder, passed it by. What a triumph when I came up with this winner especially when Mr. Ed Carson, who has been gathering information about Homer Laughlin over the years, let me copy an ad from Albert E. Sloan, Inc. in Chicago who in 1953 offered china in these patterns. Each set purchased would include a "free gift" of a teapot, creamer and sugar. I noticed in the ad that the flatware shows several different Currier & Ives pictures that are different from the one that is on the casserole shown below. In powder blue, this pattern is called* **Blue Heaven**.

Plate 54

Plate 55

Plate 56

Virginia Rose, which was produced beginning in 1929 and was sold for home use into the 1970's, was possibly the most popular shape ever created by HLC. An entire plant (Plant #8) was devoted primarily to the production of Virginia Rose. The shape was named for the granddaughter of Mr. W.E. Wells, who was responsible for setting the course of development of the company in its early days. She was also the sister of Mr. Joseph Wells, Jr., another member of the dynasty which has held management responsibility of the company for almost 100 years. When I visited the factory in 1991, I was told that this lady had only recently passed away.

Virginia Rose was widely distributed through a number of channels. It was sold by department stores, the largest seller of which was Woolworth's. It was also sold through other stores such as Wards and Sears. It was given as premiums in conjunction with trading stamp programs such as Plaid Stamps. It was sold via catalog through distributors such as Cunningham and Pickett, and Vogue. Finally, it was given away as premiums with Quaker Oats and to patrons of movie theaters. In view of the vast amounts of this shape that were produced, it is a wonder that more of it is not seen in antique shops today.

The shape is characterized by a rose motif embossed into the rims of all of the pieces (Plate 58). This embossed rose was repeated different numbers of times depending on the piece. Plates have six repetitions of the rose. Serving dishes have four repetitions (two on each side) with a different embossed design on the ends. Cups have the embossing around the rim. The hollowware serving pieces have a well-developed foot. The lids of the sugar and casserole are distinctly raised in the center, with fluted handles.

Although Virginia Rose was supplied with an almost limitless variety of decorative decals, the predominant decoration appears to have been pale pink roses with pale green foliage. The more interesting decals are much less common.

I have been less successful in obtaining the pattern names of Virginia Rose. In the literature available to me, it appears to have simply been sold as 'Virginia Rose" and nothing more. I had hoped to obtain additional information on this subject from Woolworth's, who was one of the larger distributors. Unfortunately, they have been of little help, apparently having neither the archival records nor the interest in documenting today what was certainly a very important time in their history.

*Plate 59: Pattern **HLC #JJ59**. This pattern is the most familiar of all the Virginia Rose patterns. I see it for sale in many antique stores and swap meets, and it is shown in both Jo Cunningham's and the Huxfords' books. I was not able to find a name for this pattern but the decal number I found at the Homer Laughlin factories indicates that it was sold through J.J. Newberry's. Shown: 10" plate, sugar with lid, cream, cup and saucer, and double egg cup. (Photographed by Norman Nossaman, from the collection of Darlene Nossaman.)*

Plate 57

Plate 58

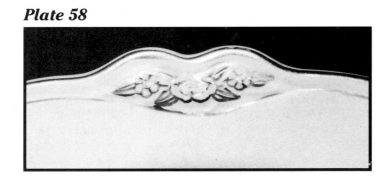

Plate 59

Plate 60: From right to left: **Nosegay** *Pattern HLC VR 423 on a 10" plate. This pattern is pictured in the 1941 Sears catalog. Middle: Patrician, on a 9" plate. This simple decoration of platinum outlining of the embossed roses of the Virginia Rose shape also came in gold. Although I had heard the names* **Silver Rose** *(for the platinum) and* **Gold Rose**, *I found the name Patrician in a reprint of the 1934-1935 Larkin Soap catalog. Left:* **Bouquet** *Pattern HLC W137. The "W" in front of the HLC pattern number indicates it was a pattern exclusive to Woolworth's. I found the name in the archives at the HLC plant in a file of patterns sold to Woolworth's.*

Plate 61: Pattern **HLC #VR 135**. *This was a popular decal that was also used on the Century and Yellowstone shapes. Shown are the 13" dish (platter) and the sauce boat. This decoration stands out from so many other nondescript Virginia Rose floral patterns in that the colors are more intense, and that only a single group of flowers is used.*

Plate 62: The cream, sugar with lid, and saucer are shown in the Pattern **HLC #VR128**. *This is a very familiar pattern which is often seen on Virginia Rose. The 13" dish (platter) in the Pattern TEMP VIRG 194 combines the use of flowers with the platinum outlining of the Virginia Rose embossing to achieve a very striking effect. A narrow stamped band appears around the verge. The use of the platinum outlining on the embossing provides an excellent example of the special treatment accorded the handles of the platter. These details are ordinarily very hard to see in a photograph.*

Plate 60

Plate 61

Plate 62

Plate 63: These Virginia Rose salad bowls were decorated in three different colors: blue, green and red (not shown). The colored pattern is quite thick, and appears to have been put on with a stencil. The decals in the bottoms of the bowls were added separately. I have a couple of pages from a Homer Laughlin brochure on specialty items (dating probably from the 1950's), which shows these bowls with an identification number of **HLC #W1700**. Considering the HLC practice to assign consecutive numbers to variants of the same decoration which differed only in color, it may be assumed that this number referred to one of the available colors and that the others were numbered 1701 and 1702. This brochure also shows other unusual items such as a lobster platter (with a large picture of a lobster), a spaghetti bowl, and a snack plate.

Plate 64: This Virginia Rose nappy was decorated with Pattern **SAL 74**. There were also **SAL 73** (Green) and **SAL 75** (Blue). These are shown in another brochure of specialty items from the 1950's period. This brochure also advises the purchaser that the overall size of the nappy was 9¾", and that they came packed in lots of 3 dozen (consisting of one dozen each of the three colors.) This same brochure also shows salad bowls which were 9" and designated as NY or New York Salads and PA or Pennsylvania Salads with a wide green or yellow band around the rim and a decal in the center. It also shows a turkey platter (with a picture of a turkey in the center) and jumbo-sized coffee cups with "Father" and "Mother" on them.

Plate 65: Pattern **HLC #VR396**. This pattern, which I've heard called "Tulips in a Basket," features red and yellow tulips in a yellow basket, and seems to be an easy pattern to find. Shown are the 8" baker and the sugar with the cover.

Plate 63

Plate 64

Plate 65

Marigold

The Marigold shape, to me, represents something of a discovery. My husband, having visited a local antique shop on my behalf in a never-ending quest for HLC china, came home lugging a beautiful HLC platter with a stylized flower petal embossed into the china. The cluster of petals were contained in pronounced scallops about the edge of the piece, rather in the style of Virginia Rose. Having consulted my available reference materials without success, I photographed the piece. When I was subsequently able to discuss the photo with some people at the HLC factory, the mystery was solved. Mr. Joseph Wells, Jr., whose connection with the company extends back for several decades, told me it was called Marigold. Marigold, I was told, was brought out at the same time as Virginia Rose, and appears to have been completely overshadowed by the success of its competitor. Marigold used a special light-yellow glaze called Marigold Glaze. According to Mr. Thiemecke, this was a low thermal expansion glaze originally developed for the "Ovenserve" line. It used oxides of uranium to achieve its unique color. With the advent of World War II, the uranium oxides became unobtainable, and the glaze formula was altered to use a mixture of oxides of iron and titanium to create the original color. This glaze was subsequently used on Virginia Rose as well.

Having given Marigold its proper name, we now have found that pieces of it were turning up rather often in the local shops, although the hollowware (except for serving bowls) seems to be rather rare. The platters are oval in shape, with the characteristic Marigold scallop appearing six times around the margin. The round dinner plates have five scallops. There are also square plates, with a scallop in each of the four corners.

The heavily embossed five-petal pattern (Plate 67) is carried forward to the hollowware as well. The teacups have the pattern appearing around the rim, with four repetitions of the pattern. The cups and saucers have a solid feel about them, rather like Nautilus, but not as heavy as Century. The cream and sugar continue the Marigold theme. The cream and sugar have a sort of Grecian shape, with curled-up handles. The first thought that came to mind upon beholding these was some of the commercial art by Maxfield Parrish.

As far as casseroles, lids, and the like, I haven't a clue as to what they look like. My guess is that when you find them, they will each bear an unmistakable imprint of the five-petal Marigold motif somewhere in a prominent place. Happy Hunting!

In my travels through the local shops, I have on several occasions encountered Marigold being offered as Virginia Rose. The mistake of a careless or uninformed seller can reward the astute collector, who can obtain the prize at a fraction of its worth. Look carefully at that next piece of Virginia Rose, and see if instead of roses it has marigolds. You may have found yourself a deal!

Plate 66

Plate 67

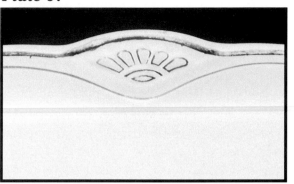

Plate 68

Plate 66: An example of the Marigold backstamp sometimes found on pieces of Marigold china. Be warned that the plain garden variety HLC backstamp is found more often than the Marigold backstamp.

*Plate 68: On the left, a cup and saucer in **Pennsylvania Dutch** pattern. These pieces carry the American Vogue backstamp, and have a hand-painted look. On the right is an 11" dish (platter) in the Pattern **HLC #M207**. This decoration is typical of many seen on Marigold, consisting of small flower bouquets around the rim, which is edged in gold. The pattern number was obtained from a matching plate found at the HLC factory.*

Plate 69: Some very elegant samples of the Marigold shape. They are all characterized as being empty of decoration except for the highlighting of the edges and the Marigold embossing with precious metal. On the left are a 13" dish (platter) and a cream decorated in platinum Pattern TEMP MARI 203. On the right are a 6" plate and sugar (with no lid) with gold decoration Pattern TEMP MARI 209.

Plate 70: A 15" dish (platter) in a very unusual decoration consisting of a bright red coloring of the Marigold embossing with a small black dot at the base Pattern TEMP MARI 204. The combination of the bright red and the fan-like appearance of the colored embossing lends an oriental feel to this piece. I would very much like to find more of this pattern.

*Plate 71: A rimmed soup and 9" baker in the Pattern **HLC #M-90**. The use of the green to set off the Marigold embossing creates a very simple and pleasing effect. This decoration scheme is virtually identical to one I have seen on Virginia Rose.*

Plate 69

Plate 70

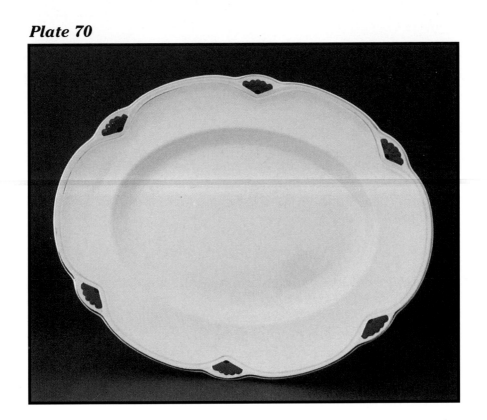

Plate 71

*Plate 72: Pattern **HLC #M212** on the 12" dish (platter) and dated on the back in 1945. At first I thought this was the same pattern as the one shown in Plate 73. On closer inspection, I found that M212 includes tulips, and that the flowers are arranged in a slightly different way.*

*Plate 73: **Springtime**, Pattern **HLC #W245**, dated 1944. This lovely pattern with its large bouquet of pink, white, orange, and blue flowers was sold by Woolworth's. It must have been quite popular, because it is much easier to find than the other Marigold patterns. Shown are the 9" plate and the nappy.*

*Plate 74: Two 8" square plates. The plate on the left is decorated in Pattern **HLC #M208**. The one on the right is in **HLC #M201**. At first glance the two decorations appear to be identical. However, a closer examination will reveal that the flower arrangements are different (although if you encountered a written description of the flowers I doubt if it would be possible to tell which of the plates the description referenced.) The gold stampings on the verges are also subtly different. The Marigold shape appears to have been the recipient of similar but not quite identical decals rather often compared to the other HLC shapes.*

Plate 72

Plate 73

Plate 74

Wells is one of the most interesting and unusual shapes to emerge from the HLC factory, and certainly deserves consideration as one of the most artistic. It is quite ornate in design, compared to other HLC creations of the time, yet not distastefully so. The shape was designed by Frederick Rhead and was sold beginning in 1930. It should be noted that there is some confusion in the use of the name "Wells" to describe both the shape and the vellum glaze that was developed at the same time. Any piece (so far as I know) that used the Wells glaze will carry a backstamp showing a peacock and the word "Wells." This backstamp does not identify the shape, but to my knowledge the peacock appears on all pieces of Wells shape. Thus, if the piece does not bear the peacock, it is not Wells. If the peacock is present, then it could be Wells, but it could also be Century or Jade. All of this confusion aside, it is the shape rather than the glaze that is the subject of our attention here.

Unfortunately, it is impossible to date individual pieces of Wells since the backstamp deviates from the usual HLC scheme in that it contains neither the company logo nor any dating information. The name "Wells" obviously was given to commemorate one of the Wells family so closely associated with HLC since the beginning. The shape was probably named for W.E. Wells, Sr., the very same man that took over the company for Homer Laughlin himself back in 1897, and who died in September 1931. This theory is subject to some question, since the Wells shape was originally sold to Wards without a name, and was then given the formal name "Wells" to honor W.E. Wells after his death in 1931.

The Wells shape seems to have received an unusual share of the HLC creative talents, in that not only is the shape itself notable, but it also received the special attentions of Dr. Bleininger, the noted ceramics engineer who was the technical director at HLC at the time. Initially the shape was glazed in solid colors (matte green, peach, and rust.) Later came the famous vellum glaze, which is a matte ivory color. The unique texture of the vellum glaze, according to Mr. Thiemecke who worked with Dr. Bleininger, was achieved through the use of titanium oxide, while the coloring of the glaze was obtained with oxides of uranium.

The handles of the cups, teapot, coffee server, etc. display a sort of "winged spiral" motif which is heavily embossed into the side of the handle. The pieces with lids have handles which continue this motif, this time expressed as a "loop on top of a loop," with the spirals pointing toward each other. The shapes of the pieces themselves are quite simple and functional, with a sort of grace about them that is difficult to describe. The shapes of the flatware pieces are not as striking, although the 8-inch square plates with their distinctive octagonal outline and circular wells will certainly catch the eye. The rim of the platter has a decided concave curve to it. Regardless of the details of the shape, look out for the vellum glaze and the unique backstamp of the peacock.

Plate 75: TEMPWELL 210. The ad for this set, in the 1936 Montgomery Wards catalog reads, "76-Piece Matched Table Service. Complete service for 6: $7.95." This set of Wells dishes with the green trim came with matching crystal (goblets, sherbets, and salad plates) and a large set of silverware. Shown: 9" plate and 11" dish (platter). (Photographed by Norman Nossaman, from the collection of Darlene Nossaman.)

*Plate 76: **Gold Stripe**. Also from the 1936 Wards catalog is the ad for this Wells pattern with "soft ivory color and a gold line on the outside edge of each piece and a narrower gold line inside." Shown: 9" plate, 7" plate, fruit, sugar/without lid, and creamer. (Photographed by Norman Nossaman, from the collection of Darlene Nossaman.)*

Plate 75

Plate 76

Plate 77: Pattern TEMP WELL 212. This muffin cover and 8" plate, with its exceptionally pretty pink and blue flower decal, was another treasure that I obtained from Mike and Lorna Chase of "Fiesta Plus."

*Plate 78: **Flowers of the Dell** shown on the 8" square plate. This pattern is described as "sprays of blue, purple, green, and brown flowers" in the 1930-31 Wards catalog page shown in Jo Cunningham's book.[8] After looking at this pattern in her book for several years, it was a delight to finally see it in living color on a shelf in an antique shop, and to realize that it was the same as the picture shown in the old black and white catalog page.*

*Plate 79: Pattern **HLC #W8523** is shown on the casserole, 8" square plate, and 13" dish (platter). This Arts and Crafts style decal of orange and yellow flowers with green and black leaves fits very well on the Wells shape. This decal is also found on other HLC shapes, and from what I have heard, was used by other china companies as well.*

Plate 77

Plate 78

Plate 79

Century

The Century shape began production in the early 1930's, probably 1931. Century is unusual for two reasons: first, each piece was basically square or rectangular, and second, Century pieces were covered with the special vellum glaze which gave it a decidedly matte texture. The effect of this glaze, which is suggestive of old ivory, is quite pleasant even in the absence of other decoration. Altogether, the feeling of Century is pure Art Deco.

The pieces of the Century shape are noticeably massive. Virtually all of the pieces have a square or rectangular appearance. Bowls and plates have round wells. Platters have oval or rectangular wells. Platters also have a sort of handle or tab on each end, embossed with several parallel lines. The hollowware pieces are footed. The handles on cups, cream and sugar, and the the cream soup bowl are unusual in that they have a sort of scalloped top edge. These features should enable one to easily recognize Century in a moment.

The Century shape appears to have been quite successful, judging from the number of different retailers (Sears, Wards, Larkin) who sold it and the relative ease with which it can be found in antique stores today. The shape was graced with a wide variety of decorations, including simple rings and bands, various floral and geometric designs, and scenes with a decided theme to them. In the latter category was a variety of Mexican patterns. Finally, the Century shape was used as a basis for the Riviera pattern of solid color glazes. Both the Riviera pattern and the Mexican patterns have been amply covered by the Huxfords in their book[9] on Fiesta™ ware.

We have noted that the quality of the Century available today is non-uniform. We find pieces whose workmanship is flawless, and we find others which appear to be seconds or thirds – plates which will not sit flat on the table and pieces whose edges are obviously warped. According to people I spoke to at the HLC plant, they were experiencing problems in their manufacturing methods in this time period, which may explain some of the quality problems.

*Plate 80: Pattern **HLC #C24**. This set with the very unusual pattern of large black and silver flowers almost seems to be hand-painted, but I've seen the decal in the Homer Laughlin pattern book. The tops of the handles and the edges are decorated in platinum. It also has a bright, multi-colored peacock backstamp indicating the use of the famous Wells vellum glaze. (Plate 85) Shown: 11½" dish (platter), 7" plate, 9" baker, fruits, 9" plates, and cup and saucer.*

*Plate 81: Pattern **HLC #C22**. On a deep vellum glaze are three green lines, placed on the verge of the plates, platters, and soups, a half-inch down from the top of the hollowware pieces, and in bands on top of the handles. The nappy that fits so well with this set (but is not actually a part of it) is the **English Garden** pattern, sold by Sears Roebuck and appearing in their 1933 catalog. It is interesting to note that the HLC #C22 pieces all display the peacock (denoting the use of Wells vellum glaze) in silver, (Plate 86) while the English Garden displays the peacock in colors. I specifically questioned Mr. Thiemecke about the significance of this difference and was told that there was none. However, he also told me that any backstamp in a metallic color would have been put on over the glaze, and would have been subjected to a third, low-temperature firing.*

In addition to the English Garden 8" nappy, the pieces in the HLC #C22, pattern include: cup and saucer, 11½" dish (platter), 9" plate, 9" baker, fruits, and rimmed soup.

Plate 80

Plate 81

Plate 82: **Old English Scene** *is what the Huxfords'[10] call this pattern. Shown in the photograph is the 13" dish (platter). I was very attracted to the fairytale-like appearance of the decoration on this piece.*

Plate 83: Pattern **HLC #JJ50** *on a 9" plate. This pattern, which was sold to J.J. Newberry's (hence the JJ in the pattern number), also appears on Virginia Rose. The cream soup cup shown with the plate is decorated with HLC decal 335. The same decal can be seen on Yellowstone.*

Plate 84: Pattern **HLC #C144**. *Shown is the 12" dish (platter) with an oval well and a baker. I was lucky enough to get the pattern number from the bottom of the baker. Transparent pink flowers and taupe-colored leaves give this set a very soft design. When taken with the vellum glaze, the result is a pleasant, muted look.*

Plate 82

Plate 83

Plate 84

*Plate 87: Pattern **HLC #C17** on the sauce boat and sauce boat stand. This pattern appears in the 1932 Sears catalog as "Century Vellum." A 96-piece set cost $28.75 back then. The decal shows flowers (perhaps gladiolas) in yellow, red, and orange, with yellow daisies. I purchased this outstanding set from Mike and Lorna Chase, of Fiesta Plus in Tennessee. They offer other unusual HLC items for sale, and advertise regularly in "The Daze."*

*Plate 88: Pattern TEMP CENT 228. This 12" dish (platter) is one of the more simple patterns that can be seen on Century. Its only decoration is a continuous gold stamp design that is shown on the rim of the platter's rim. The deep bowl (20 oz., 2½" deep x 5½" wide) is decorated in a beautiful pattern of flowers in delicate yellows and pinks, which I have labeled as TEMP CENT 229. I located this hard-to-find piece in the "Underground" in Ontario, California. The sauce boat is decorated in **Columbine**, which was identified in Huxfords[11]. It shows stylized flowers and leaves in yellow, orange, and green. The deep plate (also known as the rimmed soup) shows Garland, **HLC #C45**. It has a gold-stamped floral pattern on the rim, and a gold-stamped medallion in the center.*

Plate 85

Plate 86

Plate 87

Plate 88

Production of the Nautilus shape began in the early 1930's. Nautilus is one of the more interesting shapes to come out of Homer Laughlin. The theme for this shape is a heavily sculptured shell motif. This shell motif is boldly stated in the handles of the serving dishes, particularly the casserole and the sugar bowl. It is also echoed in the embossing on the ends of the platters and the stand for the sauce boat.

The serving dishes (sauce boat, casserole, cream, sugar) have a decidedly plum shape, which can easily be seen in Plate 90. The casserole, cream, and sugar are unusual in that they stand on small feet, rather than on a simple rim. Notice also that the handles of the gravy boat and the cream have a small protuberance on the very top.

A diagnostic feature of the plates and bowls is a double ring on the bottom (see Plate 103). Although this feature is shared by Virginia Rose, the two shapes cannot be confused since Virginia Rose has a heavily scalloped edge while Nautilus has generally smooth rims.

It is interesting to note that during the 1950's, Nautilus flatware was combined into sets with Cavalier hollowware by Cunningham and Pickett, and by Albert E. Sloan with Charm House hollowware.

*Plate 89: Pattern **HLC #W150**. This pattern seems to have been popular because I see it rather often in the antique stores. I am very attracted to patterns with large white flowers and this is no exception. It features large white Gardenia flowers set against dark green leaves and has a ½" gray band around the rim. The double eggcup has a gray band inside and a white flower bud outside. The Nautilus eggcup seems heavier than most and has a pronounced ridge around the bottom of both cups. Shown are: 13"dish (platter), casserole, and double eggcup.*

Plate 89

Pattern W-238

1 Cup and Saucer	8 Dish (Meat Platter)	15 Coupe Soup
2 Pickle	9 Cream	16 Oblong Covered Butter
3 Double Egg Cup	10 Cereal Dish	17 Nappie (Round Veg. Dish)
4 Baltimore Coffee Mug	11 Fruit	18 Sauce Boat
5 Bowl	12 Baker (Oval Veg. Dish)	19 Covered Casserole
6 A. D. Cup and Saucer	13 Plate	20 Onion Soup
7 Covered Sugar	14 Deep Plate (Rim Soup)	

Plate 90   79

Plate 91: The 6" plate is decorated with a dark red rim, gold stamp, and a picture reminiscent of paintings by the 18th century French artist, Antoine Watteau. It is hard to decide whether it should be framed or used at the table. On the back, the date is 1952 and the stamp says 22 kt. gold. This plate may be either part of a regular Nautilus set, or it may be part of a "mix and match" set like Lady Stratford and Lady Greenbrier. I have given this pattern an identification of TEMP NAUT 245.

Plate 91

Plate 92: **Lady Stratford** *and Plate 93:* **Lady Greenbriar**. *The section of this book on "Mix and Match" provides an explanation of these patterns.*

Plate 92

Plate 93

Plate 94: **Amsterdam** *pattern on Nautilus. Mr. Ed Carson of HLC told me this pattern was made by the company for the Interstate Utilities Corporation of San Francisco, California, in 1952. Mr. Carson sent me a copy of an advertisement showing this set entitled "Amsterdam Holland." While searching old records at the HLC plant, I found an old work order containing the following description of this pattern:*

> *"1 center decal, ½" wide green color band below the verge. Band inside cups and decal outside. Band dropped ⅔" on saucer. Gold edge line and slight gold handles. Foot line on cups and hollowware."*

A number of different decals were used with this set, some of which are shown here. Some of the decals have names in the picture (perhaps the name on the original painting), however I have not seen this on all of the different pictures. The pieces shown in Plate 94 are described individually below.

Plate 95: On the 10" plate the decal is a picture by Constable called "The Cornfield." It shows a shepherd boy drinking from a stream while his dog guards the sheep. The 13" platter shown has the same decal, but I cannot say whether all of the platters follow this pattern.

Plate 96: The deep plate (rimmed soup) shows a stream with trees with a bridge in the background. A woman is washing clothes in the stream, while another woman is sitting on the bank. A dog is playing in the stream.

Plate 97: The decal on both the creamer and sugar decal is a windmill against a stormy sky. The lid of the sugar shown here is missing.

Plate 98: The decal on this 7" plate decal shows a house, stream and trees. A couple in a small boat follow cows in the stream.

Plate 99: The special Amsterdam backstamp used with this interesting pattern.

Plate 94

Plate 95

Plate 96

Plate 97

Plate 98

Plate 99

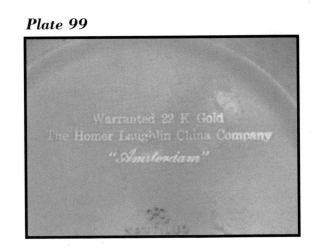

Warranted 22 K Gold
The Homer Laughlin China Company
"Amsterdam"

Plate 100: **Cardinal***. This pattern consists of small red flowers and black leaves sprinkled over its surface. The same pattern can be seen on Swing in Plate 161, where it kept the same name.*

Plate 101: In the right foreground is a sugar (with no lid) in the **Magnolia** *pattern. It has large white flowers edged in pink set against yellow-green leaves. The cream and the 9" plate are decorated in the colorful* **Colonial** *pattern. Note that the decoration on the cream has been truncated to just the floral group, bracketed by the bold dashed lines. The wide blue band on the rim is similar to those appearing on so much of the Brittany.*

Plate 102: **Bouquet***. This set shows both the HLC and the Cunningham and Pickett backstamp. It has the more ordinary decal of a floral bouquet showing pink and yellow roses, blue and orange flowers, and green leaves. I can easily see this as a grocery store premium for which Cunningham and Pickett were known distributors.*

Plate 100

Plate 101

Plate 102

Plate 103

Plate 103: Details of the bottom of the Nautilus flatware, showing the double ring marks which are characteristic of Nautilus. Note also the backstamp, which is not to be confused with the backstamp for Eggshell Nautilus described in a later chapter.

Plate 104: An advertisement for Nautilus which appeared in the October, 1936 issue of China, Glass, and Lamps. Although HLC predicts that "Early America bids fair to be one of the most popular patterns that Homer Laughlin has ever produced," I have yet to find my first piece of this very attractive pattern. I would dearly love to possess a set of Early America, or even a single piece.

Plate 104

October, 1936

3

Early America
by
HOMER LAUGHLIN

THIS "Early America" pattern is one of those delightful adventures in decoration which appeals to the imagination of prospective customers, whether their tastes run primarily to the traditional or the modern in tableware.

Naive, delicate and unusually pleasing, this creation is in the spirit of Duncan Phyfe . . . and yet it is as modern as tomorrow. Its reception at the recent House Furnishing Show indicates that "Early America" bids fair to be one of the most popular patterns Homer Laughlin has ever produced.

THE HOMER LAUGHLIN CHINA COMPANY - NEWELL, W. VA.

Pacific Coast Representative: M. Seller Co., San Francisco, Calif., and Portland, Ore.

Chicago Office: Room 15-104, Merchandise Mart

I first heard of Coronet through Lois Lehner's book[12]. There was no clue, however, as to what it looked like. My first view of Coronet was at the HLC factory, when I traveled there with Darlene Nossaman to collect material for this book. After I returned to California and began to gather material for the book in earnest, I ran across an advertisement in *The Crockery and Glass Journal* for March 1935 that devoted a full page to Coronet. However, I had still not seen any in the shops I had visited. Coronet, as can be seen in the illustrations, is decidedly unlike what could be regarded as the main line of HLC designs. Consequently, it would be easy to pass it by, thinking it was china by another maker.

I was able to find a platter in Palmdale, California. Therein lies a story: After having found the material on Coronet in the trade journal, I was most anxious to find a piece for my own collection. On a particular Sunday afternoon my husband and I drove out to the desert to check out some shops in an area where we had never been. As we drove out, he remarked to me that he felt in his bones that a piece of Coronet would be found that day. Sure enough, in the third or fourth shop we went into, he found the platter shown in Plate 105. Since that first find I have found little other **Coronet** in Southern California, the most significant find being an almost complete set at Captain Kidd's in Ontario, California. Unfortunately, I was not able to photograph this set in time for inclusion in this book. In my opinion, the **Coronet** shape should be regarded as somewhat rare.

Coronet was created in the same time period as Virginia Rose and Marigold. It appears to have been completely overshadowed by these more popular shapes, and thus never sold very well. The following description of Coronet is taken from an unidentified trade magazine, which was published when the shape was first announced:

> "The latest arrival in shapes at the Homer Laughlin China Co. is the Coronet. The covered dish is tall with a fluted base and a wide band of fluting around the top of the bowl, the cover offers a knob bearing out the height of the piece. The handles are double and are drawn right from the center of the body and modeled so as to bring out the fine lines in the body. The fluting is not the ordinary run – rather it is a series of folded flutes, one over the next, with a smart braiding and floral combination to hem it in. The plate which is rather flat, uses the fluted treatment for the rim. The cup has its fluting around the rim, and a handle which is thin and yet sturdy enough for usage."

Coronet was offered in a plain ivory glaze, as well as with various colored treatments (the HLC advertisement refers to "old ivory, sea green, and ming yellow") and decorations.

Plate 105: This is the Palmdale platter that was my first Coronet acquisition. It clearly shows the diagnostic elements of the shape: the pronounced fluting that covers the rim of the flatware, and the braiding that appears on the inside of the rim. This platter is probably in the Old Ivory glaze mentioned in the extract from the trade magazine. The fact that this piece is otherwise undecorated allows the embossing to be fully appreciated.

Plate 106: These were pieces I discovered tucked away at the HLC factory, where they had lain undisturbed for the decades since they were made. The photo was taken under very adverse conditions, for whose quality I apologize. My husband insisted I include it because it shows the details of the lid and handles of the casserole. The handle on the lid bears a resemblance to the same handle on the Wells casserole. The handles on the body of the casserole are also quite elaborate. The sides of the casserole provide an excellent view of the detail of the braided band. The interesting bowl in the background with the handles formed from extensions of the body is not identified. I would have thought a nappy, but Plate 107 shows a nappy which clearly has no handles. I have no idea what it is.

Plate 105

Plate 106

Plate 107: A 9" nappy, also probably in the Old Ivory glaze. The nappy gives an indication of the treatment of the outer edge of the rim, which is scalloped somewhat in the manner of Virginia Rose. The fluting and the braided band along the inner edge of the fluting can be clearly seen. This piece is from the collection of Darlene Nossaman.

*Plate 108: Two coronet plates showing decorative decals. On the left is a 7" plate with an unnamed pattern I have identified as TEMPCORO 263. The interesting decoration shows a large and very realistic brown tiger lily, surrounded by other colorful flowers. On the right is a 5" plate in the **June Rose** pattern. This pattern was identified from the 1935-36 Larkin catalog. A copy of the page which shows Coronet appears in Plate 109.*

Plate 107

Plate 108

Plate 109

JUNE ROSE PATTERN

Refreshing and lovely as roses in June, this delightful, new pattern is fully as charming as its name suggests. Designed in the very newest shape, it displays against the popular ivory body a beautiful spray of large, pink and white roses and buds, interspersed with blue flowers and green leaves. The whole is most attractively set off by a lovely, embossed border. It is a set of which you will never tire, appropriate for any occasion. Its durability permits you to enjoy it in everyday use.

32 Pc. $9 COUPON VALUE

Size of Set	32-pc.	51-pc.
Number	1423	1430
For COUPONS	$9.00	$16.00
Mlg. wt.	18 lbs.	34 lbs.

(1935/36)

The Crockery and Glass Journal of April 1936 announces "The new Brittany shape." A month later, in the same publication, we find an advertisement by Homer Laughlin which shows a variety of patterns on the new Brittany shape. From this beginning, Brittany was produced until at least 1950. Brittany was sold through typical HLC outlets, including Wards, Sears, and Cunningham and Pickett. Today it is one of the more easily found shapes in the local antique shops.

Unlike some of the other shapes that came out during that period, Brittany appears quite conservative. Neither the flatware nor the hollowware display any unusual characteristics. Plates are round with no embossing or fluted edges. Hollowware pieces (of which there were two different designs during the life of the Brittany shape) are also relatively simple. The shape of the earlier hollowware can be seen in Plate 110.

The decorations on Brittany are noteworthy. First, there is an endless succession of decals of the type shown in Plate 110 through 114, which superficially look the same. A careful comparison of the similar maroon (or blue) bands in these similar patterns will reveal differences in the decorations at the ends of each colored segment, in the presence of various decorative elements embedded in the colored band, such as flower shapes, heart shapes, etc., and in the presence or absence of a floral group in the center of plates and platters.

Second, there is another entirely different type of decoration to be found on many samples of Brittany. This is a silk screened pattern which was applied before the piece was glazed. HLC called this the "Under-glaze Silk Screen" line. Examples of this type of decoration can be seen in Plate 117.

Plate 110: **Majestic, HLC #W538** *in red and* **HLC #W638** *in blue. Majestic was the name Woolworth's gave this pattern. The hollowware for this pattern changed to the new style somewhere along the line. Shown: deep plate (rimmed soup), sauce boat, cream, and sugar (but without its lid.) The opposite page shows the HLC advertisement for these patterns.*

Plate 110

Plate 111

THE HOMER LAUGHLIN CHINA CO., NEWELL, W. VA.

Patterns W-538 and W-638

1 Cream	5 A. D. Cup and Saucer	9 Cream Soup Cup
2 Covered Sugar	6 Nappie Cover	10 Fruit
3 Dish (Meat Platter)	7 Nappie (Round Veg. Dish)	11 Plate
4 Cup and Saucer	8 Deep Plate (Rim Soup)	12 Bowl

*Plate 112: Right: 10" plate in the Pattern TEMP BRIT 272. The ends of the maroon border are V-shaped, with a small heart shape at the apex of the "V." In the center is a 6" plate showing the Pattern **Rosewood HLC #B1314** in which the maroon bands have gone off into a fantasy of curlicues. On the left TEMP BRIT 273 is another 10" plate, whose decoration is distinguished by a continuous narrow band of tiny shapes at the very outer edge of the rim.*

*Plate 113: Pattern **HLC #B1315**. This pattern, which is almost identical to the one in Plate 110, was only one of a series of Brittany patterns that closely resembled one another. Close examination shows this pattern has different flowers in the insert, the scallops around the flowers is shaped like a single letter "C," rather than the double "C" scallop appearing on Majestic. Finally, there is no flower decal in the center of the flatware pieces. These slight differences are all that separate two entirely different patterns. Shown: 14" chop plate and cream.*

*Plate 114: A 13" dish (platter) in the **Clive** pattern, which was shown in the Montgomery Wards catalog from the 1940's. Note the cleanly cut ends of the colored band segments and the presence of little flower decorations within the colored band at each end. Also shown is a saucer with the less common blue bands decoration. This pattern TEMP BRIT 274 is quite ornate.*

Plate 112

Plate 113

Plate 114

Plate 115: A copy of an HLC advertisement from the September 1936 issue of "China, Glass, and Lamps" showing Brittany in a plaid silk-screened pattern. The advertisement tells us that this pattern style was offered in four different color schemes. We are fortunate to be able to see in Plate 115 what one of these (B1201) looks like in real life. This pattern appears on the 10" plate. I believe another of these color schemes (B1205 in yellow and black) appears on page 205 of Jo Cunningham's book[13].

Plate 115

Plate 116

The new plaid patterns in four colorings are an important addition to the Homer Laughlin underglaze silk screen line.

In harmony with both traditional and modern furnishings, these gay decorative wares were accorded an unusually warm welcome at the recent housefurnishing show in New York. The color numbers are:

ROSE AND BLUE, B. 1201.
GREEN AND BLUE, B. 1202.
YELLOW AND BLUE, B. 1203.
YELLOW AND BLACK, B. 1205.

THE HOMER LAUGHLIN CHINA COMPANY - NEWELL, W. VA.
Pacific Coast Representative: M. Seller Co., San Francisco, Calif., and Portland, Ore.
Chicago Office: Room 15-104, Merchandise Mart

Plate 117: **Hemlock**. *This pattern is shown in the 1940's Montgomery Wards catalog and was still offered as late as 1956 in the Sears Roebuck catalog. There seems to be a difference in the thickness of the dishes and decal was slightly changed as the years passed. I have not seen a mention of the green color but placed them together since the decal seems identical except in color. Both dishes (platters) shown are 13".*

Plate 118: Pattern TEMP BRIT 118. This very conservative gray and white pattern has the hollowware with the wide bottom and narrow top bodies and solid round knobs. This large set was still in its original packing and in mint condition. Shown are: nappy, cup and saucers, creamer, and sugar bowl.

Plate 119: Pattern **HLC #B1055**. *This nappie's pattern was shown as part of a series of patterns featured in the June 1936* Crockery and Glass Journal. *The title read "A series of patterns in silk screen underglaze decorations on the new Brittany shape." Note that the hollowware is in the "new" style.*

Plate 117

Plate 118

Plate 119

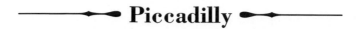

Piccadilly

When I first learned about this shape I thought there must be some mistake. I didn't think Homer Laughlin had ever made anything that looked like it. My friend Darlene Nossaman who sent me her sugar bowl to photograph had discovered the Piccadilly backstamp in Lois Lehner's book[14] and alerted me to a possible new shape. Mr. Ed Carson, the first person I asked about it, told me it was made to go with Brittany flatware. Below is Darlene's sugar, and a Brittany 10" plate that I had whose decoration seems to be an exact match. The pattern is another of the "Lady Alice look-a-likes."

On the opposite page is a picture from the Larkin Catalog reprint[15] dated 1940 which shows what is obviously a Piccadilly shape in a pattern called Empire. The Sears catalog shows Piccadilly in a pattern called Mary Ann in the years 1949 and 1950. Mary Ann was described as having "splashy colorful flowers that form a perfect center for a wide, neat, border of tiny dots."

The shape of the Piccadilly hollowware is very simple and straight in line. The handles are flat on top, and drop down in a quarter curve to meet the straight sides of the body. The lids are simple, with flattened round handles.

Based on the tiny amount of Piccadilly seen in shops (one piece, to be exact), we may safely conclude that it is somewhat rare. Because its shape departs somewhat from the more typical HLC shapes of the time, it would be easy to overlook it as being from some other potter and pass it by.

Please see the Brittany value guide for Piccadilly.

Plate 120. Pattern TEMP PICA 280. Piccadilly sugar and 10" plate.

Plate 120

Plate 121

Plate 122

Empire PATTERN

So different! Plate-rims are flat; hollow pieces have straight sides—perfect backgrounds for this wide, formal border decoration so reminiscent of the early eighteenth century. Perfect for use in period or early American dining-rooms.

This exquisitely-dainty pattern includes underglaze inlay, fluted border in Alice-blue with delicate overglaze floral sprays in near-pastels. Beautiful!

No.	Size Set	Cash or Certs.	Mlg. wt.
3074	32-piece	$ 5.95	21 lbs.
3165	54-piece	11.50	33 lbs.

The Eggshell Shapes

In the latter half of the 1930's, the Homer Laughlin China Company brought forth the Eggshell lines of dinnerware. The Eggshell wares were different from all previous designs in terms of their much lighter weights, resulting from new precision machines and tools developed by the outstanding technical team at Homer Laughlin. The result was a type of china which enjoyed a high degree of uniformity in quality which, up until that time, had not been possible. The edges of the pieces are thin and delicate. "The textures are exceptionally beautiful, and the glaze is unusually thick, uniform, and satisfying," said an advertisement in a trade publication of January 1937 which announces the new line. The new manufacturing methods, in turn, permitted the use of revolutionary artistic designs.

Beginning with Eggshell Nautilus in 1937, and followed immediately by Eggshell Georgian (both preceded by the non-Eggshell designs of Nautilus and Georgian), the Eggshell line grew during the years immediately before World War II to include the exquisitely delicate Swing (somewhat suggestive of doll dishes), and the heavily embossed Theme (designed to commemorate the World Fair in 1939). The success of the Eggshell shapes is easily seen in the relative availability of Eggshell Nautilus and Georgian in antique shops today.

The Eggshell line of Homer Laughlin china was perhaps the most successful pottery ever produced by the company for home use. In catalogs from the Montgomery Ward company of the late 1930's, through the 40's, and into the early 1950's one can find an endless diversity of patterns. During the peak of its popularity, each issue of the Wards catalog generally offered eight different patterns, four each on Eggshell Georgian and on Eggshell Nautilus. While these shapes were also offered by Sears, the choices were not as great, and Sears appeared to favor Hall China over Homer Laughlin during this period for their main dinnerware offerings.

The Eggshell shapes represented a sharp break from the earlier design efforts of Frederick Rhead, the art director at the time these shapes were first designed. While the previous shapes and decorations developed at Homer Laughlin were for the most part quite attractive, they were also stylistically tied to particular periods in time. Thus Empress and Republic (which we have already seen in earlier chapters) are quite reminiscent of the early years of the twentieth century. The delightful Century shape makes no attempt to hide its close ties to the Art Deco period. However, all of these look like antiques. If one was to set a table completely with these shapes, it would certainly cause the dinner guests to raise an eyebrow.

The same cannot be said for the Eggshell shapes. While the scarcity and fragility of Swing would discourage its use at today's table, there is certainly a strong temptation to overlook the fact that the other Eggshells are fifty years old, and to put them to everyday use. Eggshell Nautilus and Georgian particularly have a sort of timelessness about them, a sort of classic style that make them fit with almost any period. It is at times almost saddening to realize that these beautiful and completely American creations have been superseded forever by the deluge of china from Japan that began in the 1950's.

On the facing page is shown an assortment of the four original Eggshell shapes.

Plate 123

Plate 124

Plate 123 (From left to right): **Red Bell** *on Swing. Shown are the 10" plate, sugar, and cup and saucer.* **HLC #N1732,** *on Eggshell Nautilus. The decal consists of three feathers tied with a yellow bow. Shown are the 9" plate, sugar, and cup and saucer.*

Plate 124: **Regency Theme,** *with red and blue ribbons twined with green leaves. There is a matching decal in the center of the plate. There is an American Vogue backstamp along with the HLC backstamp.* **Cotillion** *on Eggshell Georgian, featuring large white flowers which were "created by the sweeping brush of the artist" according to the Sears catalog. Shown are the rimmed soup, sugar, and cup and saucer.*

━━◆ Eggshell Nautilus ◆━━

The first Eggshell shape was Nautilus, brought out in January 1937 and first shown at the Pittsburgh Exhibit of January 11-20 of that year. This first Eggshell shape, particularly in the hollowware, makes no secret of its Nautilus ancestry. Although the same basic lines of the hollowware have been preserved, the definitive nautilus-shell motif seen in the handles and acorn-shaped knobs on the lids has been refined so that this theme is simply suggested, rather than stated outright. A similar effect is seen in the handles of the platters, where the explicit nautilus-shell motif has given way to a stylized embossing which only hints at the shell pattern. In some cases, this embossing will be highlighted with strokes of gold or color. Overall, the shape radiates a feeling of solid, classic elegance.

The Eggshell Nautilus hollowware is unmistakable. The overall feeling of the hollowware is smooth, well-proportioned, and somewhat oblate. The casserole and the sugar have unique curled handles which can be immediately recognized. The soups, on the other hand, have handles more in the style of the platter, showing a reduced shell motif. The handles on the creamer and the cups have a simple ear shape. All of the hollowware shows a pronounced foot.

The flatware, on the other hand, is somewhat harder to recognize without a more careful examination. Perhaps the best identifying characteristic of the plates and saucers is the rather steep verge. In the illustrations which follow, this feature can be recognized from the shadows it casts. In most cases, the backstamp will explicitly identify the piece as "Eggshell Nautilus" (Plate 125).

The decorative patterns run the gamut from what today would be considered old-fashioned, through various floral and other pictorial representations, to simple and quite formal themes consisting of narrow lines on a background of muted color.

The demand for this shape (together with Eggshell Georgian) was undoubtedly increased by the interference of World War II with the importation of china from its usual sources in England and the Far East. Homer Laughlin did not hesitate to exploit this reduction in competition. Throughout the war years, and as late as 1950, a wide selection of different patterns was available on the Eggshell Nautilus shape.

Popular though it was, the end of its success was approaching. The decline can be seen, for example, in the Wards catalog of 1953, when only the Greek Key pattern (new in 1953) and the Nassau pattern on this shape were offered. Probably because of its widespread sales from sources such as Sears and Wards, Eggshell Nautilus is quite easy to find in antique shops today, at least those of Southern California.

*Plate 126: Pattern **HLC #1594**. This pattern is also known in some circles as "Pastel Tulip" or just "Tulip." The picture clearly shows the "Nautilus" motif embossing on the handles of the soup and the platter. Pieces shown: 13" dish (platter), fast stand sauce boat, onion soup (lug), and salt and pepper (which are from the Swing shape.)*

Plate 125

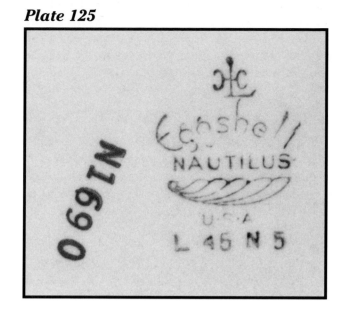

Plate 126

Plate 127: **Cardinal** *(red border) and* **Admiral** *(Blue border). These were offered in the Montgomery Wards 1938 Fall and Winter catalog. These pieces are among the most elegant I have seen from the Eggshell Nautilus line. They would be quite appropriate for a formal dinner setting. Not inappropriately, the same pattern design on Eggshell Georgian is called Monarch. Note the use of color to emphasize the embossing on the handles of the platter. Pieces shown: 11" platter and 8" plate.*

Plate 128: Pattern TEMP EGGN 293. A simple but elegant (and unidentified) pattern. The heavy gold trim on an ivory background give the pieces a classic feel. The lighting in the picture provides a good view of the shape of the steep verge of the flatware, which is diagnostic of the Eggshell Nautilus shape. Pieces shown: 7" plate, creamer, and sugar bowl.

Plate 129: Pattern TEMP EGGN 294. I found this to be an interesting geometric pattern in platinum on a white background, dating from 1936. These pieces were found in a tiny shop in the California desert area. We got to this shop on a Saturday afternoon after the proprietor had closed up and was preparing to drive away. We induced her to open up again, and these pieces are what we found. Pieces shown: 15" platter and fast stand sauce boat. (Note: "Nautilus" motif embossing on handles.)

Plate 127

Plate 128

Plate 129

Plate 130: This March 1937 ad from China, Glass, and Lamps *was of special interest because it shows six different Eggshell Nautilus patterns. One of these pictured patterns has come to life in Plate 131:* **HLC #N1402.** *In the color picture of the 13" dish (platter) the beautiful cobalt blue surrounds the flowers.*

Plate 132 (Right): **Gardenia** *on the 10" plate. This pattern was one of the top ranking prize winners in the American Vogue Dinnerware contests staged by the Vogue Mercantile Company. Left:* **Prizewinner** *Pattern* **HLC #VM112** *on the 15" dish (platter), not to be confused with the prizewinning Gardenia pattern on the right. Prizewinner is a pattern of subtle coloring, with greens, yellows, taupe, and purple leaves. Both Gardenia and Prizewinner have the backstamp of the distributor, America Vogue, along with the expected HLC backstamp.*

Plate 130

Top Row	N-1401	N-1402	N-1258
Bottom Row	N-1439	N-1405	N-1406

Plate 131

Plate 132

Plate 133 (Left): **HLC W450**. *An 11" dish (platter) with very pleasing flower decal. The "W" prefix to the pattern number indicates this unremarkable design was probably sold by Woolworth's. Right: A rimmed soup in the **Acacia** pattern. This more interesting pattern features bright yellow and orange poppies. It has the backstamp of Cunningham and Pickett.*

Plate 134: Pattern TEMP EGGN 298. A most elegant Eggshell Nautilus casserole. The pattern is similar to the flower-and-scroll bands seen on the old Empress shape. The picture provides a good look at the details of the scroll handle and the knob on the lid. It also provides a good look at what sometimes happens when the decorations are applied. Note the irregularities in the placement of the decorative band on the body.

*Plate 135: **Nantucket**, Pattern **HLC #N1753**. This pattern was identified from the Wards catalog of 1953, during the heyday of HLC home tableware. This pattern is quite modern, and could as easily grace a table today as when it was sold almost 40 years ago. I ran across this set in an antique store in Ventura, CA but passed it by when I first saw it. I was quite pleasantly surprised when I spotted the very same pattern in the Wards catalog. A quick phone call back to the antique store confirmed that they still had the set, and I immediately bought it. Shown: 10" dinner plate, 5" fruit, nappy, 7" plate, sugar bowl, rimmed soups, creamer, and saucers.*

Plate 133

Plate 134

Plate 135

Plate 136: **Aristocrat** *is the pattern name shown in the 1953 Montgomery Wards catalog. This regal pattern fits well on the Eggshell Nautilus shape and features the usual red, yellow and blue flowers but set off by intricate gold decorations against an ivory background.*

Plate 137: **Rochelle**. *This pattern appears in the 1958 Montgomery Wards catalog. I purchased some pieces of it at a flea market for a song but have been discovering other pieces at local antique stores. The gold trellis and scroll work are topped by a floral bouquet of pink and blue flowers.*

Plate 138: **Ferndale**. *This pattern of small pink roses, blue flowers and green leaves is the same decal that was used of the Eggshell Georgian "Cashmere." The pattern name comes from Jo Cunningham's book[16].*

Plate 136

Plate 137

Plate 138

*Plate 139: **Blue Dawn**. I came across this pattern pictured in the 1947* China, Glass and Decorative Accessories *trade magazine. The dishes are banded in a pale blue that looks like tapestry and outlined in tan and set in various spaces of the band are pink and yellow flowers. Shown are: saucer and sugar.*

*Plate 140: Pattern **HLC #N1690**. At first glance this lovely set has a pattern very similar to the Blue Dawn but on closer examination I found it to be distinctly different. This banded pattern feels to me like it should grace the cover of an old book. Shown are: 13" dish (platter), 9" nappy, 9" baker, sugar bowl, cup and saucers, 9" plates, creamer, and fruits.*

*Plate 141: Pattern **HLC #N1706**. An Eggshell Nautilus egg cup is the highlight of this set with a "Calarose" pattern. A band of pink is around the verge on the flatware with a large pink rose, rose buds and green leaves in the center. Shown are: 6" plate, cup and saucer, and double egg cup (Swing).*

Plate 139

Plate 140

Plate 141

Eggshell Georgian

The second Eggshell shape to be produced by Homer Laughlin was Eggshell Georgian. Like the Eggshell Nautilus before it, Eggshell Georgian appears to have been derived from an earlier non-Eggshell design. A notice in *Crockery and Glass Journal* for December of 1933 announces the initial presentation of a line called "Craftsman Dinnerware," to be shown for the first time in Pittsburgh in January of the following year. Later advertisements in the same publication (June 1934) for a pattern called Chartreuse on Craftsman Dinnerware shows what appears to be Georgian! Again in *Crockery and Glass Journal* (October 1935) is an advertisement for "Georgian Dinnnerware." Since Eggshell in any form was not manufactured prior to 1937, the Georgian of October 1935 is almost certainly a design of normal weight, although otherwise appearing identical to Eggshell Georgian.

Eggshell Georgian presents the same sort of elegant feel as Eggshell Nautilus. However, the differences between the two shapes are unmistakable. Whereas the Eggshell Nautilus shape presents a rather smooth appearance (except for the embossing on handles), the same cannot be said for Eggshell Georgian. A theme that sets this shape off from others is the unique "line and bead" embossing that appears on both the hollowware and the flatware. The plates will show this embossing around the edge of the rim (Plate 144), sometimes highlighted in gold or color. The hollowware will show the line-and-bead around the outside of the well, and again around the edge of the pronounced foot.

The most obvious feature that sets Eggshell Georgian apart is the design of the hollowware, and particularly the designs of the handles. The creamer, sugar, salt and pepper, and the coffee server all present a noble, upright stance which is quite different from the squat feel of Eggshell Nautilus. The handles on the lids of the creamer, teapot, and casserole are pierced and heavily embossed. The handles on the body of the casserole continue this theme, although these handles are somewhat rolled into a scroll shape. Finally, the handles on the teapot, creamer and sugar, and the gravy boat will have a small protuberance on the top of the handle which, with the usual application of decoration to this area of the handle, is hard to miss. Any question of the pedigree will usually be solved in an instant by turning the piece over and noting the definitive backstamp (Plate 143).

The growth of Eggshell Georgian appears to have paralleled that of the slightly earlier Eggshell Nautilus. It was heavily advertised during the 1940's (particularly after the war), at which time Wards usually offered a choice of four different patterns in each catalog. It appears, from the examination of these old catalogs, that some of the patterns would be carried forward from catalog to catalog, while others would appear in only one or two issues, and then be seen no more. Like the Eggshell Nautilus also, the fall-off in popularity appears to have been rather abrupt, with most of the choices disappearing from Wards by the middle 1960's.

*Plate 145: This picture compares normal-weight Georgian to Eggshell Georgian. On the left is a sauce boat in normal-weight Georgian with the **Formal** pattern, bearing the "Craftsman" backstamp (Plate 142). This pattern on normal-weight Georgian can be seen in the Wards catalog over a period of time ranging from 1936 to 1943. On the right is an Eggshell Georgian sauce boat in the TEMP EGGG 320 pattern. The only difference between these two pieces is in their weight. The normal-weight Georgian does not appear to have been made in significant quantities. This is the only piece I have ever found. It turned up in a small shop in Ventura, CA.*

116

Plate 142

Plate 143

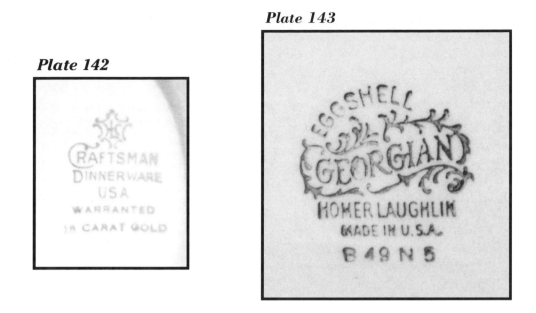

Plate 144

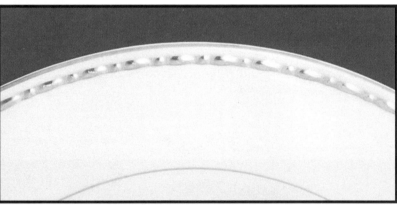

Plate 145

Plate 146: This pattern was sold by Sears in four colors. **Marilyn** *Pattern* **HLC #G3418** *is the pink seen in the 10" plate on the right. From records at the HLC plant, I found that the same decorative scheme was also available in green (HLC #G3421), yellow (HLC #G3420) and blue (HLC #G3419). Examples of the green can be seen on the 10" plate on the left, and on the saucer. The yellow variant is seen on the 8" square plate under the saucer. The flowers in the centers of the plates shown are in bright pinks, blues, and yellows, and there is a band of tiny gold fleur-de-lis around the verge. As far as I have been able to determine, only the pink variant was called Marilyn.*

Plate 147: Pattern **HLC #G3354** *(green) on the 14" chop plate, and* **HLC #G3355** *(yellow) on the 6" plate. This same pattern was also available in* **HLC #G3353** *(blue). I feel somewhat guilty about the chop plate. When I first saw it in the antique shop I knew I had to get it, because it was somewhat rare. Little did I know that another patron of the shop also had his eye on the same plate. Unfortunately he took time, as he walked about looking at other items to consider his decision. By the time he decided to purchase it, it was already mine.*

Plate 148: **Chateau** *Pattern* **HLC #G3468***. While Sears was selling the Marilyn shown in Plate 146, Montgomery Wards was selling this almost identical pattern. Wards appears to have sold only the Robin's Egg Blue sets with a similar but more subtle center flower decal of pinks and blues and a tulip. It also had a gold fleur-de-lis band around the verge. Homer Laughlin shows it being made in* **HLC #G3467** *(pink).*

Plate 146

Plate 147

Plate 148

Plate 149: **Cashmere**. *This pattern features dainty sprays of pink and yellow roses with small blue flowers on wispy branches. I ran across this now familiar pattern in the Montgomery Ward 1953 catalog. Shown: deep plate (rimmed soup) and sauce boat.*

Plate 150: **Countess**. *Pattern* **HLC #G3432** *This pattern that is found in the Sears Roebuck catalog is an almost identical pattern to Montgomery Wards Cashmere. The same description could be used for both, but a careful inspection shows it is indeed a different decal. Countess has no small blue flowers on its wispy branches, and an extra rose hangs down from the middle cluster. Shown: 9" baker and covered casserole.*

Plate 151: Salt and pepper shakers in the **Cashmere** *pattern. This picture was taken by Norman Nossaman from Darlene Nossaman's collection.*

Plate 149

Overleaf:
Plate 152: **Viceroy**. *Until I found a picture in the Montgomery Wards 1944 catalog, naming the pattern Viceroy, I had been calling it Ivory Rim because of the wording used in a Homer Laughlin advertisement which appeared in a 1940 trade magazine,* China, Glass and Lamps *(Plate 154). This elegant pattern with its ivory rim, white center and gold covered embossing was used both by itself and as a background for various decals.*

Plate 153: Left: **HLC #G3391**. *An example of an Ivory Rim pattern with a decal that is the same as on the Nautilus Ferndale. The HLC records indicate that this pattern was made for Montgomery Wards. Right:* **English Regency** *Pattern* **HLC #G3357**, *identified from the advertisement in* China, Glass and Lamps *from December 1940. Again we have the thrill of seeing an old black and white advertisement come alive with the real thing.*

Plate 150

Plate 151

Plate 152

Plate 153

Plate 154

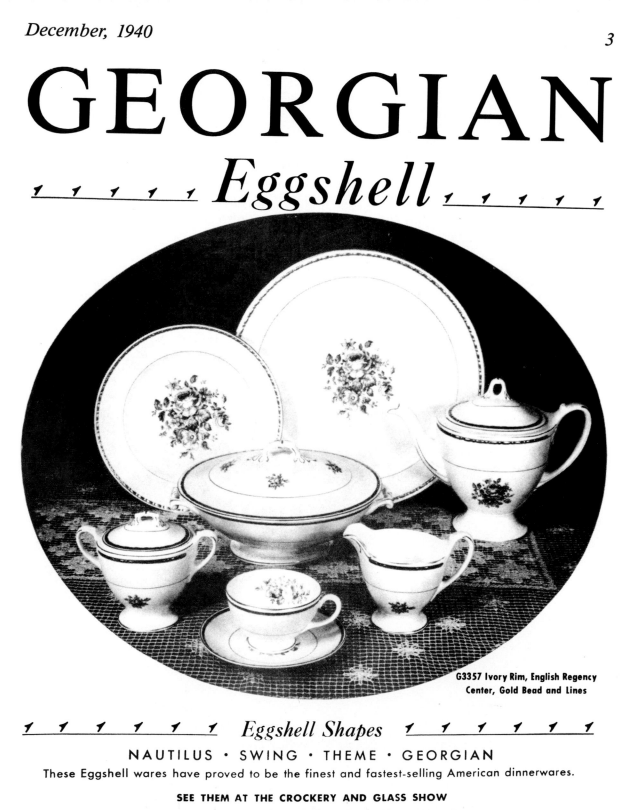

Plate 155: **Greenbriar** *Pattern* **HLC #3499**. *Decorating the rim of this pattern are decals of natural appearing green and gray leaves and rose colored flowers and berries. It has a two-tone background with a white center and ivory blending from the shoulder to the outer rim. I found the name of this pattern on a small brochure, dated April 1, 1949, given to me at the Homer Laughlin factory. In the rear of the photograph, from left to right: 10" plate, 8" plate. Front, from left to right: sugar with lid, fast stand sauce boat, cream. (Photo by Norman Nossaman, from the collection of Darlene Nossaman.)*

Plate 156: **Bombay**. *I found this pattern at the Homer Laughlin factory and photographed it on a piece of brown paper since that was what was at hand. I wanted it shown because it was shown for several years in the Sears Roebuck catalog. The copy I have is from 1949 and calls it the "modern version of the popular Indian Tree pattern." It also shows matching tumblers with the Bombay pattern on them.*

Plate 157: **Rambler Rose**. *This pattern name that was used in the Montgomery Wards catalog was also sold under the American Vogue backstamp. The pattern has small red roses and green leaves set against a snowy white background. All pieces are edged in gold. I found the Rambler Rose to be one of the more common patterns in the local antique stores.*

Plate 155

Previous Page:
Plate 154: Copy of an advertisement from a 1940 pottery trade magazine showing Ivory Rim with a decal that Homer Laughlin calls **English Regency**. *This page was photographed from an original copy of the periodical in the archives of the East Liverpool Museum of Ceramics, an excellent source of historical material about Homer Laughlin and other potters from that area.*

Plate 156

Plate 157

Plate 158

Swing

Swing was the third of the Eggshell shapes to be produced. This unusual shape is characterized by its extreme simplicity and delicacy. The impression of a Swing breakfast set is that of dishes intended for the serving of dolls, or perhaps elves. Homer Laughlin announced in the January 1938 the first showing of the new shape in Pittsburgh at the Crockery and Glass Exhibit that month. According to this advertisement, the shape was named "Swing" because it was "designed in the tempo of the times." Their words describe the shape as having "simple, smooth-gliding lines," and having "a dynamic, youthful appeal." Although Swing was offered into the 1950's, it does not appear to have been a very popular shape.

Both in shape and decoration, Swing is unmistakable. The hollowware is easily recognized by means of the unique shape of the handles on the bodies and lids. These all consist of a little, round curl, rather like one might make by rolling the wet clay around one's finger. The words used to describe the shape and feel of the hollowware would be "plump" and "extremely fragile." The sides of the creamer, sugar, cups (both demitasse and coffee), and the casserole are simply and smoothly curved. This same feel is carried into the teapot as well. The flatware also has this feeling of delicacy. However, the most definitive identifying feature of the flatware is the convex curve of the rims. These rims almost have a curl to them. If the handles and the unique shapes of the pieces have not given it away already, Swing can invariable by recognized by its special back stamp (Plate 159).

The decoration appearing on the Swing shape cover the spectrum from wide stripes in solid pastel colors, through stylized floral patterns, to decorations which consist of pictures on Oriental themes, pictures of trains, pictures with Mexican themes, etc.

Swing certainly did not enjoy the popularity of the Eggshell Nautilus and Georgian which came before it, undoubtedly because of its rather unusual appearance and its feeling of delicacy. The impression upon seeing Swing for the first time is one of wonder that all of the handles were not broken off in the first year of use. In spite of its apparent lack of utility, Swing is an absolute treasure to own. Collecting Swing is not easy, since it is quite scarce in Southern California, and it is strongly suspected that this scarcity exists in other areas as well. If a piece of Swing is encountered during an afternoon's antique hunting, it should be snatched up without hesitation, as it may be a long time before another piece is discovered. While I have purchased some directly from other collectors through periodicals such as *The Daze*, I have rarely found more one or two pieces in any of the local antique shops and shows. A delightful exception was an adventure to the antique shops of Saugus, California. There I found major parts of what had apparently been a complete dinner set of Swing, divided between two different stores. In the space of 30 minutes, I more than doubled my Swing collection. Pieces of this set, with its lime green border, white center, and Oriental decoration can be seen on some of the following pages.

Plate 159

Plate 160

Plate 161: ***Cardinal***, *sold by Cunningham and Pickett. This distributor gave the same name to the Swing as was given to the Nautilus shown in Plate 100. The backstamp says "Hand Decorated" and "Cardinal" rather than the usual Swing backstamp. However, the 8" plate with its convex curved rim is unmistakably Swing.*

Plate 162: A regal pair. On the left: ***Sovereign*** *on the 11" plate. This elegant pattern consists of a simple gold edge line with a gold fine line, and a verge line, also in gold. The name of this pattern is very appropriate. Right:* ***La Petite*** *on the rimmed soup. This pattern consists of an 18th century couple surrounded by gold stampings of large flowers and leaves, outlined in dark red above the verge line at the edge line. Besides the HLC Eggshell backstamp, there is another backstamp which I am trying to identify. It is most likely the stamp of the distributor, and consists of a large "N" with a crown above it, in gold.*

Plate 163: Some of the tiny and delicate Swing pieces. On the left are some pieces from a breakfast set in the ***Lime Organdy*** *pattern. Shown are the AD cream, AD sugar, double egg cup, 8" plate, muffin cover (which goes with the 8" plate) and the AD coffeepot. The Organdy pattern came in lime green, maize yellow, icing pink, and sky blue. Curiously, the handles were always green no matter what the color of the decoration. Note this color scheme on the* ***Pink Organdy*** *cup and saucer at the far right. At the top center appears a lone cup in the* ***Apple Blossom*** *pattern. This cup is from an after dinner set, rather than a breakfast set. Swing AD sets were sold for some time after the standard Swing dinnerware was discontinued.*

Plate 161

Plate 162

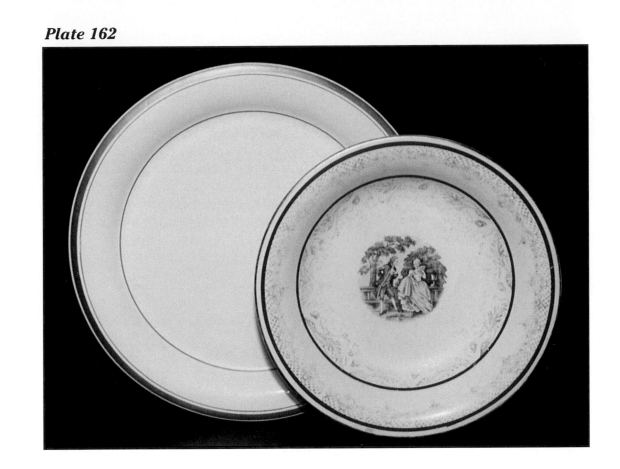

Plate 163

The following pictures will give the reader a good idea of the extensive use of decals on the Chinese theme. Shown are **Chinese Buddha** (Plate 166), **Chinese Princess** (Plate 168), **Chinese Three** (Plate 164), **Chinese Willow** (Plate 169), and **Chinese Porcelain** (Plate 170). The collection of Swing in the Chinese theme was a slow process that sort of took on a life of its own after a while. The original find, Chinese Buddha, was discovered by my husband at Rhoda's in Canoga Park, CA, which always seems to have some kind of HLC treasure stashed away each time we visit. The Chinese Three pattern is from the collection of Darlene Nossaman of Waco, TX, and was the next find. Darlene and I discuss our finds on an almost daily basis. Then came Chinese Princess, the great booty from Saugus I mentioned. The last two pieces pictured here, Chinese Willow and Chinese Porcelain, I discovered in the archives of the HLC factory. Since good close-up photos of the decals are available here, I will not take the trouble to provide detailed descriptions.

Plate 164: Details of the Chinese Three decal.

Plate 166: Shown: 9" plate, cup and saucers, fruit, and 9" baker.

Plate 168: Shown: 15" dish, (platter), cup and saucer, 11" dish (platter), 7" plate, sauce boat and sauce boat stand, oatmeal, fruit, and creamer.

Plate 164

Plate 165

Plate 166

Plate 167

Plate 168

Plate 169

Plate 170

Theme

Theme was the last of the original Eggshell series to be designed by Frederick Rhead. It was produced beginning in 1939, thus coinciding with the opening of the World's Fair in New York. It is quite different in appearance from most of the predecessor HLC shapes, being virtually encrusted with an embossed raised flower and fruit design. While the basic shape and embossing of Theme are quite eye-catching, it is quite easy to mistake certain shapes brought out by Wedgewood of England for HLC Theme. Unfortunately for the collector of Theme, Wedgewood seems to be much more common, so that what at first appears to be a find turns out, when the backstamp is examined, to be a disappointment. On the other hand, Theme can also be confused with another HLC shape called Orleans. Orleans is quite rare, compared to Theme. Orleans is described in another section of this book.

Theme is described in the January 1940 issue of *China, Glass, and Lamps* as being made in the Homer Laughlin ivory body and glaze. Because of its decorative embossing, HLC says that it needs no other decoration. However, it was supplied in both undecorated and decorated states. The intent of the shape appears, according to the HLC advertisements, to have been made to emulate china that was much more expensive. Thus the goal of Theme was to provide at an affordable price the appearance normally associated with china that was much more costly. Although Theme does not appear to have been as popular as some of the other Eggshell shapes, its attractiveness to the buying public was enhanced by the fact that it became the only game in town during World War II, when the European china that it was designed to emulate became unavailable in America.

Like a number of other HLC lines, Theme was sold through Sears (as well as other outlets). A Sears catalog of 1941 lists a pattern called Surrey on what is obviously Theme. The cost at that time for a 32-piece set was $4.98! Another source of Theme plates is the curious tendency to use these plates as a vehicle for countless commemorative decorations. Plates with pictures of places and events seem to abound in local antique shops.

It is interesting to note that today a version of Theme is still being made by HLC as a vitreous china product. It is a much heavier weight shape, and is called "Vintage." It is made for both the hotel and restaurant trade, and for the retail market.

Plate 171

Plate 171: The Theme backstamp.

Plate 172

January, 1940

THEME...*a stunning new*
Tableware in the old tradition

FOR the first time in the history of American pottery making, a domestic factory offers to the public a table service designed and modelled in the finest traditional manner . . . potted and styled in a fashion hitherto confined to only the more expensive wares . . . and yet available at prices no higher than those of average tablewares. This new ware is called Theme, and represents another achievement by the Homer Laughlin China Company.

It is made in the famous Homer Laughlin Eggshell Ivory body and glaze. Its dominating decorative motif is a beautifully modelled fruit border. It is complete and exquisite without any other decoration. But for those who prefer delicate verge border or center decorations, a number of carefully selected patterns which harmonize with the lovely shape are available also.

A table setting of Theme in your store will attract the eye and the interest of all who see it . . . because this service, in any of its decorations, is a unique and beautiful thing. Women of taste, unable to afford wares of this type before, can now buy a distinguished table service at a popular price.

SEE *Theme* AT THE SHOW

Theme, in its various patterns, will be on display at the Pittsburgh Pottery and Glass Show, Hotel William Penn, Rooms 491, 495, and 499F. Be sure to see it!

THE HOMER LAUGHLIN CHINA COMPANY - NEWELL, W.VA.

*Plate 173: (Right) Pattern **HLC #TH11**. The decal of purple tulip and assorted pink, white, yellow and blue flowers was used on several other HLC shapes. Shown here are an 8" square plate and some 6" plates. Left: Pattern **HLC #TH6**. This decal of yellow daisies and other pink flowers reminds me of a painting by Van Gogh. Shown are a 9" plate and a saucer. While Theme seems harder to find than some of the other Eggshell shapes, I've seen both these patterns on large sets. A word to the new collector: one set for sale in an antique mall near Los Angeles Airport was badly chipped and highly priced. You may be tempted to purchase such a set anyway, thinking you'll never see it again. However, it has been my experience that if you keep looking you will find another which is in good shape. Besides, the hunt is half the fun!*

*Plate 174: A cup and saucer in the **Cameo** pattern. This is an appropriate name for this all-white, undecorated pattern, which offers no colored competition to the ornate Theme embossing. I came across the pattern name written on the front of a plate in the archives of the HLC factory. The deep plate (or rimmed soup) and the sauce boat display **HLC #TH19**, another of the flowered patterns used with Theme. This particular pattern consists of pink roses and a tulip around which are sprinkled blue flowers.*

Plate 175: These pieces of Theme, from the collection of Darlene Nossaman, are decorated with an unnamed decal of an adobe building with an indian in front. The selection of the colors yellow and blue for a southwestern motif is certainly innovative, to say the least. The designation of this interesting pattern is TEMP THEM353. Shown (from left to right): fruit, 9" plate, a sugar (without a lid), and an 8" plate beneath the sugar.

Plate 173

Plate 174

Plate 175

The Debutante shape is actually a member of an entire family of shapes, the first of which appeared as "Jubilee" in 1948 with solid color glazes. Shortly afterward, in keeping with the continuing experiments of HLC with different decorative schemes, another version of the basic shape was made which used colored clays to achieve a decorative effect. Two colors were used: "Skytone" used blue clay, while "Suntone" used brown. These striking colors set off the unique handles, which were made of a snow white clay. Skytone and Suntone were further decorated with decals which were typical of the 50's. The variant of the shape actually called Debutante by HLC appears in a Sears catalog in 1948. In September of 1950, we find the advertisement for Debutante (displaying a decal called "Champagne") in *China, Glass and Decorative Accessories*. Debutante is made and decorated in a more conventional manner, with typical HLC decals on a glazed white background. In summary, then, when you find the basic shape:

- If it has a solid colored glaze, it is called Jubilee. It was named in commemoration of the 75th anniversary of the company, and was sold in 1948 or later.

- If it is made of a blue colored clay, with snow white handles, then you are dealing with Skytone, made in the same time period, but probably after Jubilee was first released. If made from terra cotta clay, then you have Suntone.

- If it has a more or less conventional appearance, with typical HLC decals on a white glazed background, it is Debutante.

The first thing about the basic shape that catches the eye is the style of the handles. These appear to have been extruded from a cake decorating device, and then stuck on the pieces while still wet. The handles on the lids of the sugar, coffeepot, teapot, and casserole look like small versions of the cup handles. Except for the handles, the shape is rather simple and streamlined. The flatware pieces are essentially timeless, with a slight turned-up edge. The hollowware pieces, with the exception of the coffeepot, have a simple conical shape.

Although Debutante is shown in the 1948 Wards catalog (two different patterns, called Debutante and Dogwood), it does not appear to have been sold in any great quantities since it is so rare in antique shops.

Plate 176: A HLC advertisement from the August 1950 issue of China, Glass, and Decorative Accessories, *which features Debutante in the* **Flame Flower** *pattern. By this time,* China, Glass, and Decorative Accessories *had superseded the venerable* China, Glass, and Lamps.

Plate 176

Flame Flower

... another bright new pattern to grace the famous DEBUTANTE *line*

Flaming chinese red flowers and subtle gray-green leaves play across a snow white background to make this an exciting achievement in truly contemporary design.

The smartly styled DEBUTANTE shape, already a nationwide favorite with discriminating hostesses, is offered in many other beautiful decorations, all at moderate cost.

The Homer Laughlin China Co.

NEWELL, WEST VIRGINIA

Plate 177

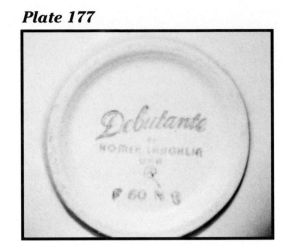

Plate 177: Homer Laughlin Debutante backstamp.

Plate 178: Shows the various pieces which make up the Debutante shape. By now, the butter dish (of which there were sometimes several varieties in older sets) has disappeared completely, and the entire set of china has been reduced to a mere 25 different pieces (counting the salt and pepper separately). However, the egg cup is still retained. With each of the pieces is shown its price (probably to the distributor rather than to the eventual user).

*Plate 179: **Wild Grapes** Pattern **HLC #D5**. The "snow white" glaze used on Debutante is set off to perfection by these decals of bright red grapes and dark green grape leaves. The pattern was sold by Sears Roebuck in 1950.*

Plate 178

STARDUST . . . Sparkling white blossoms, gracefully placed on a soft blue background, suggest a clear, cool summer night, and lend a fresh appeal to the already popular Skytone. To complete the effect, white handles and platinum trim lines furnish just the right accent. **Pattern No. HLS 180**

PIE PLATE, 7"- .35

LUNCHEON PLATE, 9"- .50

DINNER PLATE, 10"- .60

CHOP PLATE, 15"- 1.75

BREAD & BUTTER PLATE, 6"- .30

A.D. SAUCER .20

TEA SAUCER .20

COVERED TEA POT- 2.35

CREAM PITCHER- .90

A.D. CUP- .35

TEA CUP- .45

COUPE SOUP, 8½"- .50

FRUIT, 5½" - .20

COV'D. SUGAR- 1.75

COVERED COFFEE POT- 2.35

PEPPER- .65

FAST STAND SAUCEBOAT 2.65

LUG SOUP- .50

SALT- .65

ROUND VEGETABLE, 7½"- .90

COVERED CASSEROLE- 3.50

OVAL PLATTER, 15"- 2.20

OVAL PLATTER, 13"- 1.30

OVAL PLATTER, 11"- .75

EGG CUP- .50

Plate 179

Plate 180: Pattern TEMPDEBU 362. The white flower decal on this set of Debutante can be seen on the Liberty shape on page 55. What is not visible from the photograph is the faint tinge of pink that is in the folds of the petals. Shown: nappy, 10" plate, creamer, sugar, and fast stand sauce boat.

Plate 181: Pattern TEMPDEBU 363. I would have called this decoration (or rather lack thereof) "Suntone," except that the name applied to all china made with this beautiful terra cotta clay. Note that the handles, like all Suntone handles, are snowy white. Even without decoration, the rich brown color of Suntone, set off by the contrasting white would be wonderful to own. In addition to the handles, the brilliant white also appears in the knobs, the bottom half of the double egg cup, and the white plate that is under the fast stand sauce boat. Shown here: the 10" plate and the cup and saucer.

*Plate 182: **Marcia**. The blue clay of Skytone makes a perfect background for the white flowers and dark blue leaves of this pattern. The pattern name was found in the 1956 Sears Roebuck Fall and Winter catalog.*

Plates 180, 181 and 182 were photographed by Norman Nossaman, from the collection of Darlene Nossaman.

Plate 180

Plate 181

Plate 182

Plate 183

Plates 183 & 184: Pattern TEMPDEBU 366. *This special set with its gold flower stamping and heavy coat of gold on the handles, spouts, and knobs caught my eye at an antique mall in Saugus, CA. Dr. and Mrs. Roger Eckblom, in whose booth I saw it offered for sale, were kind enough to bring it 60 miles to my home in Agoura so that I could photograph it. The teapot, sugar, and cream have the Debutante back stamp. The unusual bowl with the handles and lid (which may not be Homer Laughlin at all) carries the "KAROL CHINA" backstamp. The tidbit tray carries both this backstamp and a Rhythm backstamp. My guess is that this set originated with blank pieces of china which HLC sold to a specialty company (in this case Karol China), who applied this interesting and valuable decoration. It is interesting to note that the Eckbloms, on the way to my house, stopped by a local swap meet where they discovered only one piece of HLC china, the tidbit tray shown in the photograph! How strange to come by such an unusual set in the first place, and then to find a tidbit tray (themselves somewhat rare) in the same pattern.*

Plate 184

The Cavalier shape was produced beginning in the 1950's, all the way into the 1970's. It was designed by Mr. Don Schreckengost, and was decorated in a pleasing manner with various combinations of solid colors and decals. Cavalier is a troublesome shape to the collector, since sets were made up with Cavalier hollowware combined with flatware from several different other shapes. Cavalier did have its own flatware, but this was so similar to Brittany in all but the most minute details (such as a ¼" difference in the width of the rims) that it is quite difficult to distinguish between them. A better way to tell the difference between Brittany and Cavalier flatware is that the latter is of the lighter, eggshell weight.

If you think you are home free with Cavalier hollowware, think again. The Cavalier hollowware, according to HLC documentation, included the following pieces from other shapes:

Cereal/Soup: Charm House shape
AD Coffee Cup: Jubilee shape, with special handle
AD Coffee Saucer: Swing shape
Salt & Pepper: Jubilee shape

The overall impression of the shape is distinctly modern and clean. The flatware (regardless of the shape to which it traces is ancestry) consists of simple rounds and ovals, with well-defined wells and sharp verges. An exception is the square salad plate. The hollowware pieces have smooth, curved sides and distinct cylindrical feet. Lids are smooth and slightly raised in the center, with easy-to-grasp knobs for handles.

One of the significant features of Cavalier was the use of solid colors in its decorative schemes. Many of the sets used a red, green, or blue solid color on the rims of the flatware, and as bands around the bases and the lids of hollowware.

Plate 185: This page from a HLC brochure, shows the pieces that were available in the Cavalier shape.

Plate 186: Somerset (HLC #CV87). This pattern consists of sprays of wheat, blue flowers and gray leaves banding the wide rims of the flatware and hollowware. The name of this pattern came from a Homer Laughlin catalog. Shown: 10" plate, 13" dish (platter), fruits, creamer, and the nappy.

Plate 185

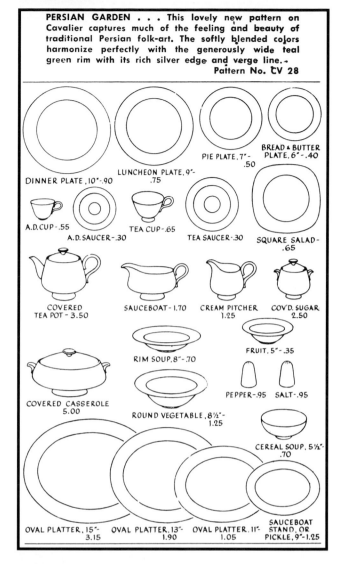

PERSIAN GARDEN . . . This lovely new pattern on Cavalier captures much of the feeling and beauty of traditional Persian folk-art. The softly blended colors harmonize perfectly with the generously wide teal green rim with its rich silver edge and verge line.

Pattern No. CV 28

DINNER PLATE, 10"-.90

LUNCHEON PLATE, 9"-.75

PIE PLATE, 7"-.50

BREAD & BUTTER PLATE, 6"-.40

A.D. CUP-.55

A.D. SAUCER-.30

TEA CUP-.65

TEA SAUCER-.30

SQUARE SALAD-.65

COVERED TEA POT - 3.50

SAUCEBOAT-1.70

CREAM PITCHER 1.25

COV'D. SUGAR 2.50

RIM SOUP, 8"-.70

FRUIT, 5"-.35

COVERED CASSEROLE 5.00

ROUND VEGETABLE, 8½"-1.25

PEPPER-.95   SALT-.95

CEREAL SOUP, 5½"-.70

OVAL PLATTER, 15"-3.15

OVAL PLATTER, 13"-1.90

OVAL PLATTER, 11"-1.05

SAUCEBOAT STAND, OR PICKLE, 9"-1.25

Plate 186

Plate 187: **Berkshire**, *from an HLC brochure, and from the June 1953 issue of* China, Glass, and Decorative Accessories. *According to the brochure, Berkshire has "a rich teal band and dubonnet and bronze-colored flowers and leaves."*

Plate 188: Left, **Crinoline** *pattern on a 7" plate. This pattern was advertised by HLC in* China, Glass, and Decorative Accessories *(date unknown). I also have this very attractive flower decal on Rhythm. Right, another 7" plate with the Lily of the Valley pattern. The name of this pattern was obtained from records at the HLC factory.*

Plate 189: **Regal Red**, *distributed by the Century Service Company. This shape has a red rim with white leaves and branches. The appearance is somewhat cameo-like.*

Plate 187

Plate 188

Plate 189

Plate 190: **Springtime**. *The June 1955* Crockery and Glass *trade journal had this to say about Springtime:*

"This new dinnerware pattern captures forever the impossible lovliness of early spring. Dainty pink and gray blossoms blend gracefully with a soft-pink band."

Shown: 9" plate, cups, and saucers.

Plate 191: The patterns shown in this photograph are quite similar. Right: **Turquoise Melody**. *Darlene Nossaman has a 1967 McDonald's Plaid Stamp catalog that shows this pattern. The blue rim with delicate flower decals was another favorite used on Cavalier. Left:* **Romance**. *From an HLC ad, "Full turquoise rim band is important background for border of dainty and delicate pastel leaves and pink buds. Every piece edged in Platinum." Photo taken by Norman Nossaman, from the collection of Darlene Nossaman.*

Plate 192: **Turquoise**. *This familiar pattern has the Lifetime China Company backstamp. Darlene Nossaman and I each had one shaker. She was kind enough to send me hers to keep mine company in this photo. Shown: 12" dish (platter) and salt and pepper.*

Plate 190

Plate 191

Plate 192

Plate 193: **Cameo**, *sold by the Lifetime China Company. The casserole, decorated in the classic Cavalier style, with a wide colored band and a large flower decal. This piece shows a band in teal green and a large rose decal.*

Plate 194: **Gray Dawn**, *sold by the Lifetime China Company. This company was a part of the Cunningham & Pickett Company, one of the largest distributors of HLC china from the 1930's through the 1960's. Gray Dawn looks almost identical to the pattern on the casserole above, except for the color of the band. I purchased a partial set in this pattern from my daughter's wedding shower. I am still on the lookout for additional pieces to complete it, particularly serving pieces. The section of this book on "Mix and Match" sets provides additional information about the Lifetime Company patterns.*

Plate 195: The nappy and fruit in the **Empire Green** *pattern, showing the wide green rim and large pink flower. The decoration on the teapot is the same except for the color of the band. Not surprisingly, this pattern is called* **Empire Gray**. *Cavalier in these patterns was sold by the Century Service Corporation, which was also a part of Cunningham & Pickett. The list of Century Service Company patterns also includes:* **Empire Red, Teal Green, Starlite Blue, Venetian Rose,** *and* **Emerald**.

Plate 193

Plate 194

Plate 195

Cavalier hollowware was often used in sets that had flatware of other shapes. The reasons why this was done are discussed in the section entitled *Problems in Identifying Homer Laughlin China*. The illustrations which follow show examples of hybrid sets made up of Cavalier, with added pieces of the Nautilus and Rhythm shapes.

Plate 196: **Jaderose** *(with the green rim) and* **Burgundy** *(the red rim). These patterns have Nautilus flatware and Cavalier hollowware. One diagnostic feature of the Nautilus flatware is the ring on the underside. The detail of this ring can be seen in Plate 103. The colored band on these pieces comes down past the verge. Shown are the 10" plate and fruit (both Nautilus) with the sugar and cream, which are Cavalier. Both of these patterns seem to be easily found in local antiques stores, a sign of its popularity. These patterns were sold by the Lifetime China Company. Other patterns offered by Lifetime China included* **Imperial**, **Gray Dawn** *(Plate 194),* **Pink Rose**, **Turquoise** *(Plate 192),* **Fieldcrest**, **Cameo**, *and the sets shown below.*

Plate 197: **Autumn Gold**. *This set uses Rhythm rather than Nautilus flatware and Cavalier hollowware (including all of the interesting orphans from other shapes, in this case Eggshell Nautilus cups). Autumn Gold is sometimes found with both a HLC and a Lifetime China backstamp, and other times with the Lifetime China stamp only. This pattern was probably distributed as a grocery store promotional item.*

Plate 198: **Gold Crown**, *another set similar to Autumn Gold. When I first acquired these pieces, I first placed them in the Rhythm section of this book. Darlene Nossaman, who also has a cup and saucer, had placed this under Cavalier in the description of her collection. I then realized I was dealing with a "mix and match" set consisting of Rhythm flatware, Cavalier hollowware, and Eggshell Nautilus cups (on Rhythm saucer). In the photograph, the plate and saucer are Rhythm, and the cup is Eggshell Nautilus.*

Plate 196

Plate 197

Plate 198

━━━━•➤ Rhythm ➤•━━━

The Rhythm shape was produced for a rather limited time, from the late 1940's until the late 1950's. It was very modern in appearance, with a simple, flowing look. The flatware pieces are either simple rounds or ovals, with absolutely no embossing or breaks in the smooth borders. The bowls look very much like the flatware, except they are deeper. The general impression of the shape is very much like Swing, but rather more sturdy and functional. One of the outstanding characteristics of the Rhythm shape is its use of the coupe shape in the plates and bowls. The coupe shape has no separately defined rim and well. The sides of the piece simply descend in smooth curve into the well area.

The Rhythm shape was designed by Mr. Don Schreckengost, and was the first to be put on the automatic jigger equipment at HLC. Initially it was made exclusively for F.W. Woolworth. Later on it was made for Newberry, and then for Wards, Sears, Pearl China Company, and Cunningham and Pickett, to name but a few. Perhaps this large distribution network explains the wide availability of the Rhythm shape, in spite of its limited period of production.

An interesting characteristic of the Rhythm shape is the decorations which were applied to it. In addition to the wide variety of attractive decals which were applied in a more or less conventional manner, HLC also used a process called "Duraprint," which involved the printing of a pattern onto the piece using an inflating rubber bladder. It should also be noted that the sets which were decorated in Duraprint used a different set of hollowware serving pieces (except for the sauce boat) than did the Rhythm decorated with conventional decals. Not only did these serving pieces have a distinctly different shape, but they were decorated in solid colors as well. Compare the shape of the conventionally decorated hollowware shown in Plate 200 with that of the Duraprint hollowware seen in Plate 210.

*Plate 199: This pattern is called **White Flowers**. I found the name and a picture of this pattern in the HLC brochure. This pattern was made expressly for J.J. Newberry Co. Shown here are the 11½" dish (platter), the cream, and the covered sugar.*

Plate 199

CAPRI . . . Delicate touches of flamingo pink to the sweeping curves of the stylized black line drawing, give a refershing sophistication to this new and sparkling dinnerware pattern. On the popular Rhythm shape.

Pattern No. RY 172

DINNER PLATE, 10"- .65

LUNCHEON PLATE, 9"- .50

SALAD PLATE, 8"- .40

PIE PLATE, 7"- .35

TEA SAUCER - .25

TEA CUP - .45

BREAD & BUTTER PLATE, 6"- .30

COVERED TEA POT - 2.40

CREAM PITCHER .90

COV'D. SUGAR - 1.80

CEREAL SOUP, 5½"- .50

SAUCEBOAT - 1.20

ROUND VEGETABLE, 8½"- .90

COUPE SOUP, 8"- .50

WATER JUG, 2 qts.- 2.00

COVERED CASSEROLE - 1.80

FRUIT, 5¼"- .20

SALT - .65   PEPPER - .65

OVAL PLATTER, 15½"- 2.25

OVAL PLATTER, 13½"- 1.35

OVAL PLATTER, 11½"- .75

SAUCEBOAT STAND, OR PICKLE, 9"- .90

Plate 200

Plate 201 & 202: **A Friend in Need** *and* **Poker Sympathy**. *Blanks were sold to the Pearl China Company, who then put on these pictures. The backstamp (see Plate 201) shows both "Rhythm" and "Pearl China Co." My husband remembers seeing large pictures of these same poker-playing dogs on the wall in a barber shop where he got haircuts when he was a boy.*

Plate 203: **Red Apple HLC #JJ150.** *This pattern was made for the J.J. Newberry Company. Shown: 13" dish (platter) and the nappy.*

Plate 204: Right: **Sunrise HLC #240**. *I found the name Sunrise in a Homer Laughlin advertisement. I also saw this same pattern for sale in the 1960 Wards catalog under the name Rhythm. The effect of the wide yellow band and the yellow wheat against the green leaves is quite striking. Shown here is the 10" plate.*

Left: **Golden Wheat** *on the 10" plate. The decal was manufactured by the Commercial Decal Company (still in operation today) for Homer Laughlin.*

Plate 201

Plate 202

Plate 203

Plate 204

Plate 205: **Rubaiyat**, *shown in the August 1956* Crockery and Glass Journal. *This HLC advertisement says:*

> *"This exquisite new dinnerware pattern blends the romance of early Persian design with the smart sophistication of today. Delicate black lines enriched by lovely turquoise and pink accents – reflect the enchanting quality of eternal beauty. RUBAIYAT – the perfect choice for gracious dining!"*

From left to right: 7" plate, cup and saucer, 10" plate, sugar with lid, and cream.

Plate 206: The pattern identification of **HLC #RY155** *came from the bottom of the nappy, a place where the official HLC pattern number can often be found. The white glaze and the simplicity of the pattern bring out the graceful vine with orange flowers and green leaves. Shown in the picture are the 15½" dish (platter), 9" nappy, and the teapot. The picture is misleading, since it makes the teapot appear to be a little larger than the cream. The problem comes from the platter, which is relatively large. The teapot, in fact, is sufficiently large to provide after dinner tea to a table-full of diners.*

Plate 207: Several sauce boats and a cream in floral patterns. On the left is **Pink Magnolia**, **HLC #RY122**. *These large pink flowers were easy to identify from a list I found at the Homer Laughlin factory. The plates are decorated with three very large pink magnolia blossoms that completely fill the center. The pattern was originally put on the Charm House shape. The sauce boat in the upper right portion of the picture shows Pattern* **HLC #W350**. *The pattern number indicates it was done up for Woolworth's. The pattern consists of sweet pea flowers. Perhaps it was sold under that name. The sauce boat on the bottom right has a decal* **HLC #RY165** *of medium sized white flowers, tinged in pink, with muted green leaves. I was able to obtain the HLC pattern number from a full set which was offered for sale (at an outrageous price) at a shop in Grover City, CA.*

Plate 205

Plate 206

Plate 207

The Duraprint process consists of printing designs on the bisque china, rather than applying a decorative design by means of painting or with decals. It allows the design to be placed under the glaze, thus giving it a longer life. It also appears to me that it would be much more amenable to mass production methods than the hand application of individual decals. According to Don Schreckengost who created the name, the process known at HLC as Duraprint arrived there from Argentina. One of his students saw this technique of printing on china while he was in South America, and brought it to Don's attention. He also had photographs which showed how the process worked. Patents were obtained for the use of the process in the USA. It was called Duraprint because it created a durable design, which was printed onto the china.

Basically, the process made use of an inflatable balloon or bladder which pressed against the piece to be decorated when air pressure was applied to it. The design itself was contained in a thin metal plate which was punctured with tiny holes in the form of the design. The colors to be applied bled through these holes in the form of the design.

The Duraprint process created a unique family of designs, which were constrained by the application process, but which could perform feats that were difficult or impractical for other decorating methods. For example, the printing could not be easily applied to sharply curved or to convex surfaces. The coupe shape of the Rhythm flatware was thus ideally suited to the application of Duraprint designs. Please note, however, that the hollowware pieces such as the cream and sugar were invariably decorated in solid colors. It was simply not possible to get such a printing device to wrap around such a piece. On the other hand the Duraprint patterns, often as not, stretched uniformly from one edge of the piece to the other. The plaid patterns shown in the Wards advertisement on the opposite page clearly illustrate this.

This and the following pages show a few examples of Duraprint, which enjoyed its own special backstamp, shown in Plate 208.

*Plate 209: Mr. Ed Carson, who retired from HLC in 1987, gave me a copy of an advertisement for Duraprint that appeared in the Wards catalog (year unknown.) It provides a good look at the scope of the shapes and the uses of both solid and patterned decorations which were applied using the Duraprint process. This pattern is called **Highland Plaid**. The hollowware is from the Charm House shape, whose flatware resembled that of the Cavalier shape. Charm House enjoyed only a limited production, but the shape of its hollowware lent itself well to the application of the solid colors employed with Duraprint. The Charm House shape had its own distinctive backstamp, which was not used when the pieces carried Duraprint patterns.*

Plate 208

Plate 209

OPEN STOCK FOR "HIGHLAND" ... SEMI-PORCELAIN

Pictured here are all the open stock pieces available in your dinnerware pattern. If you wish to increase the size of your set, add extra serving pieces or replace breakage, this will help you select.

TO ORDER OPEN STOCK. Refer to Wards big General Catalog for Catalog Number and Prices. Send your order to nearest Ward Mail Order House, or, go to any Ward Catalog Office or Retail Store. NOTE: Small dinner plates are furnished with 20- and 32-Piece Sets; large dinner plates are furnished with 53-Piece Sets.

1. Platter, Medium (about 13½ inches long)
2. Platter, Small (about 11½ inches long)
3. Bread-Butter Plate (about 6⅛ in.)
4. Salad-Dessert Plate (about 7¼ in.)
5. Dinner Plate, Small (about 9¼ in.)
6. Dinner Plate, Large (about 10⅛ in.)
7. Sauce Dish
8. Vegetable Dish, Round Open

9. Soup Dish
10. Tea-Coffee Server
    (holds five 5-oz. cups)
11. Vegetable Dish, Covered
12. Cup
13. Saucer
14. Salt and Pepper
    Shakers

15. Cream Pitcher
16. Sugar Bowl
17. Gravy Boat
18. Gravy Boat
    Stand

Montgomery Ward

86 HL 1653

163

*Plate 210: Shown here are some Duraprint flatware pieces in the **Highland Plaid** pattern. There was also a similar Duraprint pattern called Dundee Plaid. I have never seen any of it for sale, although its appearance is so like Highland Plaid that I might have overlooked it. A careful comparison of the two styles will reveal that there are slight differences in the appearances of the stripes.*

*Plate 211: A Duraprint tidbit tray in the **Confetti** pattern. The pattern consists of a regular pattern of black dots on a snowy white background, and is one of the patterns that was applied by stamping with an inflated bladder. There is a general problem with tidbit trays, in that some of them were made up by hobbyists and other similar folk who bought dishes off the shelf, drilled holes in them, and assembled them with a handy kit. These are, of course, less interesting to the serious collector. My husband spotted this piece in another one of our favorite HLC sources, Nicholby Antiques in Ventura, CA. He was going to put it aside as an imitation but I remembered seeing it in the Ward's catalog of 1956. Our notes (his notes, in fact) describe Confetti as "as array of black dots on white." The Wards catalog sold this piece separately from the regular set of dishes in the Confetti pattern. It is interesting to note that the Ward's Catalog also showed a pair of square ashtrays in black wire stands, the style being very typical of the 1950's. I don't remember if these were sold separately or together with the tidbit tray. However, one should be on the lookout for them, as I would guess they would be quite rare.*

Plate 212: A Duraprint pattern consisting of pale blue flowers interspersed with gray leaves, very typical of the fashions of the 1950's.

Plate 210

Plate 211

Plate 212

The quantity of different shapes produced by HLC over the years is truly amazing. To the beginning collector, Homer Laughlin means Virginia Rose, Century, and Eggshell Nautilus. However, as you begin to comb antique shops and to read books by other collectors, it becomes apparent that there are many more shapes than you first thought. It seems that no matter how deeply you look into the past of HLC, the bottom is never found. That has certainly been my experience. The shapes described in this section should be considered rare to extremely rare.

How did I learn of these shapes? In some cases, I came across names (with or without descriptions) while searching through pages and pages of old trade publications and HLC advertisements from the past. In other cases, I purchased a dish which I thought was a more common shape, only to find that it was something else I had never seen before when I subjected it to closer scrutiny. Some of these shapes I only uncovered when I was able to poke through a room at the HLC factory that was filled with old dishes from the past.

Jade

For several years I've had a small HLC plate on my kitchen wall, but had no idea what it was called. It was vaguely reminiscent of Century (but obviously not Century), and had a decoration with definite ties to the Mexican decorations used on Century. I was finally able to identify the shape from the Huxford's book as "Jade." I subsequently saw the same pattern on Jade in the Ward's catalog of 1934 and was able to identify the pattern on my plate as "La Hacienda." My plate was dated 1933.

The design for the complete set of Jade pieces shows a very close relationship to Century. In fact, the Jade butter dish was used with not only Century but with other shapes as well (i.e. Nautilus). An original, hand-drawn design for Jade shows the cream and sugar as being almost indistinguishable from Century. The general outline of the hollowware serving pieces is the same. However, it will be noted that Jade lids have knob handles, while Century lids have open loop handles. The Jade handles have a smooth, upward thrusting top part, while Century have a sort of bump on the top. The ability to distinguish between Century and Jade is quite important, since Century is relatively common, while Jade is somewhat rare and, thus, more valuable.

Jade used a special glaze with a slight greenish cast (hence the name?) called Clare de Lune. It was said to get its color from the presence of copper and chrome.

I was eventually able to obtain some additional pieces from an antique dealer on the East Coast, but it was quite costly.

Plate 213

Plate 214: **HLC #J7**. I will have to keep searching until I find the name of this very interesting pattern. The detail is exquisite. Lorna Chase who owns Fiesta Plus and who sold these pieces to me said someone else had bought them through mail order but returned them because they were not the Mexican patterns which he was collecting. I can't imagine ever returning such a treasure. Shown: 10" plate, fruits, and cup and saucer.

Plate 214

I bought a sugar bowl (Plate 215) at Captain Kidd's Antique Barn in Ontario, California. Beyond the backstamp, it was an unidentified shape. It is heavily embossed with a pattern of roses. I subsequently saw the same sugar (and a creamer) in Jo Cunningham's book on American Dinnerware[18] where it appears with no identification in a photograph on page 206. I was able to identify this shape as "Orleans" when I showed the photographs to Mr. Ed Carson, who retired from HLC as Office Manager in 1987. I was also able to obtain a picture of more of the pieces of Orleans. The hollowware pieces all have the embossed band of roses, and handles whose shapes closely approximate that of the human ear. The flatware continues the theme of embossed roses (two kinds – opened and closed) around the rims. The rims themselves have scalloped edges, with the scallops corresponding to the positions of the rose groups. Orleans used an ivory glaze.

Orleans appears to be quite rare. On top of that, it is quite easy to mistake it for Ravenna, whose description follows.

Plate 215

Plate 216

53 Pc. Dinner Set
No. 0-20

1- Open Sugar

1- Cream

8-4" Plates

8- Cups
8- Saucers

1-8" Dish

8- Fruits

8- 7" Plates

1- 7" Nappy

1- 7" Baker

8- 6" Deep Plates

Ravenna is mentioned in Lois Lehner's book of marks[19] where the backstamp is shown. Ravenna is a heavily embossed shape similar to Orleans. I bought a small platter, thinking I had found a highly prized piece of Orleans. When I got it home and examined it carefully, it became obvious that it could not be Orleans since the embossing, while similar, just had too many differences. The Ravenna embossing consists of groups of blossom pairs, with the blossoms appearing to just be in the process of opening. Orleans, on the other hand, has both opening blossoms and fully opened blossoms. In addition, the groupings of the blossoms are different for the two patterns. I was only able to pair the name with the design when I examined some old china at the HLC factory.

Possibly the most striking feature of the plate I bought was the design of the verge. The verge drops sharply to the well, which is flat. The slightly concave verge is marked by an embossed pattern of closely spaced vertical lines. The rim is slightly concave, with the outer edge decorated with embossed scrolls centered on the rose designs. The shapes of the hollowware pieces of Ravenna and Orleans show more pronounced differences, especially in the handles. Whereas the Orleans handles are quite ear-shaped, those of Ravenna (according to a rather incomplete hand drawing) are larger and simpler in design.

Ravenna, like Orleans, appears to be quite rare. Shown below is a 11" dish (platter).

Plate 217

━━◆━Old Roman ━◆━

Old Roman is perhaps the rarest of all. I have never seen it outside of the factory, nor do I know of anyone who owns a piece of Old Roman. I was first told of it by Mr. Carson when I visited him in May of 1992. I subsequently encountered it in the flesh at the HLC factory, when I was able to look through some old plates which had been stored away. The HLC people again were of great assistance when they let me photograph one of the plates, which appears in Plate 218.

I do not know if Old Roman was ever sold, although there is certainly ample evidence at the HLC factory that a complete set of this shape was produced and photographed. In the storage room, I found a stack of Old Roman plates with a variety of different decorative patterns. Unfortunately, no one who I was able to interview remembers the Old Roman shape. If it was ever sold, it certainly does not appear to have been in any quantity.

The striking feature of Old Roman is the embossing, which consists of a very busy pattern of interlocked scrolls reminiscent of the patterns seen on columns of Roman buildings. The piece I have has an exquisite glaze which serves to highlight the embossing. The plate appears to be far too elegant to eat from, and instead seems like it should be used as a purely decorative object. The backstamp of my plate says "Wells Art Glazes," which places it in the 30's. The round plates and the platter have the same general shape as Newell and Liberty, especially in the area of the outer edge which is scalloped in the same general pattern as the more common shapes. The sugar and cream are generally shaped like those of Liberty, further evidence of the relationship between Old Roman and Liberty.

Old Roman should be regarded as an extremely rare shape. Since I don't know if Old Roman was ever sold, I have not provided a price list in the Value Guide.

Plate 218

I first became aware of Trellis when my colleague Darlene in Texas obtained an unidentified HLC plate. I remembered seeing a shape like she described in a book on Larkin China[20] and was, thus, able to identify it as Trellis. I have found it in a shop only once. I show one piece, a small plate which appears to be a production sample, which is at the HLC factory (Plate 219).

If one examines Trellis, the impression is very much one of the Newell shape with some added features. The outer part of the rim of the plate shows the same gadroon edge, and the same pattern of scallops that are seen on Newell. The cream and sugar have the same basic shape as their Newell counterparts. The main difference between Newell and Trellis is that the latter has a repeated pattern of stylized trellises of two types: one of them has a cross-hatched motif, while the other has a pattern made up of repeated half-circles. This same trellis then is repeated under the spout of the cream.

The sparse indications that are available suggest that Trellis is one of the older shapes. The one piece that I have been able to examine has a backstamp which carries a date of 1921. The symbol for the plant which made the piece corresponds to Plant #4, which was built in 1907.

Trellis appears to be another rare shape. On the opposite page are shown a couple of examples of this interesting shape. Since Trellis is closely related to Newell, I have valued it 50% above the corresponding pieces of Newell.

*Plate 219: A Trellis 9" plate in Pattern **T7928**. This plate was photographed at the HLC factory. The large pattern number on the face indicates it was probably made for one of the shows where the company's wares were introduced to prospective customers.*

Plate 220: A group of Trellis pieces in a solid color which may, in fact, be the same as the "sea foam green" that was used on solid Coronet. Shown are a 9" plate, a cream, and a 7" plate. Note the shape of the cream, which is definitely related to Newell. Photographed by Norman Nossaman, from the collection of Darlene Nossaman.

Plate 219

Plate 220

ENDNOTES

1. Kamm, Minnie Elizabeth Watson. *Old China*. Published by the author in 1951. Ms. Kamm would be about 111 years old now, so it is doubtful that this book is still in publication. The only copy that I know of is in the Santa Paula (California) Public Library.

2. Kamm, Minnie. *op cit.*

3. Lehner, Lois. *Lehner's Encyclopedia of U.S. Marks on Pottery, Porcelain, and Clay.* Paducah, Ky: Collector Books, 1988.

4. Cunningham, Jo. *The Collector's Encyclopedia of American Dinnerware.* Paducah, KY: Collector Books, 1981.

5. Cunningham, Jo. *op cit.*

6. Huxford, Sharon and Bob. *The Collector's Encyclopedia of Fiesta, Fifth Edition.* Paducah, KY: Collector Books, 1981.

7. Cunningham, Jo. *op cit.*

8. Cunningham, Jo. *op cit.*

9. Huxford, Sharon and Bob; *The Collector's Encyclopedia of Fiesta, Seventh Edition.* Paducah, KY: Collector Books, 1992.

10. Huxford, Sharon and Bob; *The Collector's Encyclopedia of Fiesta, Fourth Edition.* Paducah, KY: Collector Books, 1981.

11. Ibid.

12. Lehner, Lois. *op. cit.*

13. Cunningham, Jo. *op cit.*

14. Lehner, Lois. *op. cit.*

15. Ayers, Walter. *Larkin China*. Summerdale, PA: Echo Publishing, 1990.
    This book is a collection of advertisements put out over the years by the Larkin Soap Company, who offered china (by HLC and others) as premiums for the purchase of their soap products.

16. Cunningham, Jo. *op. cit*, page 187.

17. Huxford, Sharon and Bob; *The Collector's Encyclopedia of Fiesta, Seventh Edition.* Paducah, KY: Collector Books, 1992.

18. Cunningham, Jo. *op cit.*

19. Lehner, Lois. *op cit.*

20. Ayers, Walter. *op. cit.*

Glossary

Bisque	China pieces which have received their first firing, and which have not yet been glazed. Bisque is generally rather porous and thus is not suitable for use until after it has received a glaze.
Embossed	A raised design formed from the clay body of a dish, as opposed to being applied to the body afterwards.
Flatware	Plates, platters, and the like. Generally, any flat dish.
Foot	An extension of the bottom of a dish, upon which the dish rests.
Gadroon Edge	A narrow embossed decorative pattern appearing on the edge of the rim, typically the rim of a plate. Newell, Liberty, and Trellis show this type of edge.
Glaze	The glass-like or vitreous decorative finish applied to china after the first or bisque firing. Glazes always receive a separate firing.
Hollowware	Dishes with raised sides and sometimes with covers, generally intended to contain liquids or similar substances. Bowls, creamers, sugar bowls, casseroles, cups, teapots, etc.
Matte	A dull, non-reflective glaze or other surface finish. According to *Webster's New Twentieth Century Dictionary, Second Edition*, both "matte" and "mat" are correct. We prefer "matte," and have used it throughout this book.
Over Glaze	A glaze applied over the decoration.
Rim	The outer portion of a dish, especially of a plate.
Under Glaze	A glaze applied to the fired china before the decoration is applied.
Vellum Glaze	A special matte glaze with the color of old ivory, which gave the glazed pieces a warm, rich appearance. Vellum glaze was often used on the Century and Wells shapes.
Verge	The point at which the sides of the dish turn upward from the well.
Well	The (generally flat) bottom of a dish.

HLC Collectors Directory

The following are places where the collector can either visit or write to enhance their knowledge of Homer Laughlin China.

Homer Laughlin China Co.
Newell, West Virginia
(Across from East Liverpool, Ohio)
(304) 387-1300

Plant Tours: Weekdays 9:30-5:00

Outlet Shop and Museum:
Weekdays 9:30-5:00
Saturday: 12:00-5:00

East Liverpool Museum of
Ceramics
400 E. Fifth Ave.
East Liverpool, OH
(216) 345-0098

Antiques Stores of Special Interest

Penny Pinchers
4266 Valley Fair St.
Simi Valley, CA 92063

Fiesta Plus
(Advertisement was in the Daze)
Mick & Lorna Chase
380 Hawkins Rd.
Cookeville, TN 38501

Nicolby's Antiques
404 E. Main Street
Ventura, CA 93003

Dr. and Mrs. Roger Eckblom
(805) 251-3050
Antique dealers, and owners of
that beautiful gold-covered tea set
featured in the section on
Debutante.

Rhoda's
21526 Sherman Way
Canoga Park, CA 91303

Inland Empire Antiques
126 West B Street
Ontario, CA 91762

Special Books Of Interest

Homer Laughlin
Identification Guide

Over 400 detailed descriptions of
Homer Laughlin patterns and
shapes.

Write To:
Darlene Nossaman
5319 Lake Charles
Waco, Texas 76710

Larkin China
(Catalog Reprint includes HLC)

Write To:
Walter Ayers
Echo Publishing
Box 279P
Summerdale, PA 17093

Naming and Sizing
of Antique China Pieces

The methods used to identify and size pieces of china are rooted in the history of the trade, and were certainly not chosen with the interests of the antique collector in mind. Unfortunately, it is sometimes impossible to avoid these arcane measurement systems, since often the only clue as to what a particular piece is will be found in an old trade catalog which uses these quaint terms. I found the process of learning about these old methods to be quite fascinating. Those of you who have been truly bitten with the old china bug will, I'm sure, find the information below to be most helpful.

Size Of Pieces

The different systems that are known to have been used at various times to size Homer Laughlin china include any of the following, used separately or in combinations with one another:

- *The number of pieces that will fit in a barrel, the normal shipment method in earlier times. A reference of 30's or 36's typically will designate how many of that piece will fit into a barrel. Note that the larger the number, the smaller the size of an individual piece, and hence the greater quantity that will fit into the barrel.*

- *Capacity, in ounces or pints. This measurement, of course, only applied to hollowware. This information can be particularly useful when one is attempting to determine whether a creamer is the standard variety, or an individual creamer. Volumetric measurement appears to be used only with pieces intended to contain fluids.*

- *Linear measurement, in inches. This size, however, is usually a "trade" size, and not the actual size that you will measure with your ruler. Thus a 9" baker has an actual length of 11 inches. Note that these measurements are not used to describe pieces intended to contain fluids.*

In my descriptions used in the value guide, I have attempted to minimize the sizing confusion by using volume in ounces or pints whenever referring to the size of a piece intended to contain fluids, if the information is available. Often the only way to get this information is to fill the piece with water, and then measure how much water it held. If this was not possible, and the volume is not otherwise known, the size will be in terms of inches or the number that will fit into a barrel.

Flatware measurements will be provided in inches. If the actual size is stated by HLC, then I used this size. Otherwise, I just measured the piece with a tape measure, and that is the dimension that is stated in the text.

Having dealt with the matter of sizing, one must address the trade names of the various piece shapes. These names, for the most part, are inherited from the English china-making tradition. Names such as "nappy" and "baker" are certain to catch one's attention. However, the collector must also be aware that a "dish" is in reality a platter. Below I have listed some of the trade names that will be encountered, in the value guide, together with today's common name for the piece, as well as other interesting information.

TRADE NAME	COMMON NAME and OTHER INFORMATION
Plate 4"	5" Bread and Butter Plate
Plate 5"	7" Salad or Dessert Plate
Plate 6"	8" Breakfast or Luncheon Plate
Plate 7"	9" Dinner Plate
Plate 8"	10" Large Dinner Plate
Plate, Deep	Rimmed Soup – Same as a Coupe Soup but with a rim or shoulder and used on a formal table.
Coupe Soup	Shallow, flat bowl generally 7 or 8 inches.
Cream Soup	Two-handled soup used with a saucer underneath – for an informal table.
Onion or Lug Soup	Handles are tabs instead of pierced handles – contents slightly more than a cream soup – about the size of an oatmeal.
Nappy	Round or square, uncovered vegetable bowl.
Baker	Oval, uncovered vegetable bowl
Casserole	Round, covered vegetable bowl
Covered Dish	Same as a casserole but oblong shaped instead of round.
Bowl	Round deep container
Fruit	Sauce or dessert dish
Oatmeal	Much the same as a fruit but larger, usually around 6" and used for cereal.

TRADE NAME	COMMON NAME and OTHER INFORMATION
Pickle	A small oval platter measuring about 9"
Chop Plate	A large round or square serving platter, 12 to 20 inches in diameter
Sauce Boat	Gravy Boat
Fast Stand Sauce Boat	Gravy Boat with attachee underplate
Tea Cup	Conventional size used in America for tea or coffee.
A D Cup	Small size cup for after dinner coffee.
Coffee Cup	Oversized Tea Cup generally used for serving breakfast coffee.

Value Guide

The valuing of antique china is somewhat of a subjective process, and the values shown on the pages which follow are to be taken as a guide only. The values given are for pieces in pristine condition. The values are affected by the following factors:

Decoration – Pieces which are decorated in an interesting and pleasing manner are worth more than those whose decorations are common and uninspired.

Workmanship – Pieces which are shaped as the manufacturer intended are worth more than those which are warped or otherwise misshapen. Similarly, decorations which are applied evenly and with skill will increase the value of a piece, while those which are uneven or out of place will reduce its value.

Style – Certain styles are more valued than others. At the present time, any of the rectilinear shapes (such as Jade and Century) will have increased values because they are more sought after by collectors. This is also true of shapes, and even individual pieces, which make a strong and pleasing statement of style. Examples of these are the Nautilus and Wells casseroles.

Demand – In the last reckoning, value is established by the laws of supply and demand. These rules will prevail in cases where certain shapes or individual pieces are specifically and avidly collected by groups of people. Fiesta™, with its current high values, is a good example of this effect. Individual butter dishes and bone dishes are also subject to this type of upward pressure on value.

Wear and Damage – A missing lid of a piece which was originally accompanied by a lid will reduce its value by a factor of two. A chip in a visible place will also reduce the value by a similar factor. Cracks will reduce value, the amount in proportion to the extent of the crack and its visibility. Finally, value is reduced by wear which affects the decoration. Gold and platinum are particularly subject to wear, since they are unprotected by any glazing.

In the pages which follow, suggested values are provided for each of the shapes described in this book. For each of the shapes, a complete list of all of the pieces that HLC identified as making up that shape are shown. In each of these lists, the trade names (rather than common names) are used. To translate trade names to common names, refer to the section on Naming and Sizing of Antique China Pieces.

EMPRESS

This list is from the 1927 Homer Laughlin Catalog.

Baker, (Oval Bowl) 5"	$8.00-10.00
Baker, 7"	$9.00-11.00
Baker, 8"	$10.00-12.00
Baker, 9"	$12.00-14.00
Baker, 10"	$14.00-16.00
Baker, 11"	$16.00-18.00
Fruits, 5"	$4.00-6.00
Fruits, 6"	$6.00-8.00
Bowls, Thin Oyster, 6oz.	$8.00-10.00
Bowls, Thin Oyster, 10oz.	$10.00-12.00
Bowls, Thin Oyster, 14 oz.	$12.00-14.00
Boullion Cup, 6 oz	$15.00-18.00
Boullion Saucer	$10.00-14.00
Butter, Covered	$45.00-55.00
Butter, Individual, 3"	$5.00-10.00
Cake Plate, 10"	$15.00-20.00
Casserole, 9"	$20.00-30.00
Celery Tray, 11"	$20.00-25.00
Covered Dish, 8"	$18.00-24.00
Creamer, 5 oz.	$8.00-12.00
Creamer, Individ., 4 oz.	$6.00-10.00
Cream Soup	$12.00-16.00
Cream Soup Stand	$10.00-12.00
Coffee Cup	$8.00-10.00
Coffee Saucer	$6.00-8.00
Dish (Platter), 6"	$6.00-8.00
Dish, 7"	$7.00-9.00
Dish, 8"	$8.00-10.00
Dish, 9"	$9.00-11.00
Dish, 10"	$10.00-12.00
Dish, 11"	$11.00-13.00
Dish, 12"	$12.00-14.00
Dish, 13"	$13.00-15.00
Dish, 14"	$14.00-16.00
Dish, 15"	$15.00-20.00
Dish, 17"	$18.00-25.00

Plate, 6"	$4.00-5.00
Plate, 7"	$5.00-6.00
Plate, 8"	$6.00-8.00
Plate, 9"	$7.00-9.00
Plate, 10"	$8.00-10.00
Plate, Deep 7"	$7.00-9.00
Plate, Coupe 7"	$6.00-8.00
Nappie, (Round Bowl)	$8.00-10.00
Nappie, 8"	$10.00-12.00
Nappie, 9"	$12.00-14.00
Nappie, 10"	$14.00-16.00
Nappie, 11"	$16.00-18.00
Oatmeal, 6"	$6.00-8.00
Oyster Tureen, 8"	$45.00-50.00
Pickle, (Handles) 8"	$12.00-16.00
Sauce Boat	$14.00-16.00
Sauce Boat Stand, 9"	$8.00-10.00
Fast Stand Sauceboat	$20.00-25.00
Sauceboat, Double Handle	$40.00-50.00
Sauce Tureen, 6"	$45.00-55.00
Sauce Tureen Stand	$10.00-15.00
Ladle	$15.00-22.00
Sugar, Covered, 4"	$12.00-18.00
Sugar, Individ., 3"	$8.00-12.00
Teacup	$5.00-7.00
Tea Saucer	$3.00-4.00
Teapot	$65.00-75.00
Jug, 48's, 4 oz	$14.00-16.00
Jug, 42's, 7 oz	$16.00-18.00
Jug, 36's, 11 oz	$18.00-20.00
Jug, 30's, 18 oz	$22.00-24.00
Jug, 24's, 27 oz	$26.00-28.00
Jug, 12's, 35 oz	$30.00-32.00
Jug, 6's, 42 oz	$35.00-40.00
Egg Cup, Boston	$15.00-20.00

KWAKER

This list is from the 1927 Homer Laughlin Catalog.

Page 23

Baker, (Oval Bowl) 5½"	$10.00-12.00
Baker, 8"	$12.00-14.00
Baker, 9"	$14.00-16.00
Baker, 10"	$16.00-18.00
Baker, 11"	$18.00-20.00
Fruits, 5"	$3.00-5.00
Fruits, 6"	$6.00-8.00
Bowls, Deep, 6 oz.	$10.00-12.00
Bowls, Deep, 10 oz.	$15.00-20.00
Bowls, Oyster, ¾ Pint	$10.00-12.00
Bowls, Oyster, 1¼ Pint	$15.00-20.00
Bowls, Oyster, 1¾ Pint	$20.00-22.00
Butter, Covered	$45.00-55.00
Butter, Individual, 3"	$5.00-10.00
Boullion, 6 oz	$12.00-14.00
Boullion Saucer	$8.00-10.00
Casserole, Covered	$20.00-30.00
Cake Plate, 10"	$16.00-18.00
Covered Dish, 8"	$20.00-30.00
Cream Soup	$8.00-10.00
Cream Soup Stand	$6.00-8.00
Coffee, AD	$12.00-14.00
Coffee Saucer, AD	$6.00-8.00
Coffee Cup	$8.00-10.00
Coffee Saucer	$6.00-8.00
Cream	$10.00-12.00
Celery Tray, 11"	$16.00-18.00
Dish, (Platter), 7"	$7.00-9.00
Dish, 8"	$8.00-10.00
Dish, 9"	$9.00-11.00
Dish, 10"	$10.00-12.00
Dish, 11"	$10.00-14.00
Dish, 12"	$12.00-16.00
Dish, 13"	$13.00-17.00
Dish, 14"	$14.00-18.00
Dish, 15"	$15.00-20.00
Dish, 17"	$16.00-24.00
Plate, 6"	$4.00-5.00
Plate, 7"	$5.00-6.00
Plate, 8"	$6.00-8.00
Plate, 9	$7.00-7.00
Plate, 10"	$8.00-10.00
Plate, Deep, 9"	$7.00-9.00
Plate, Coupe, 7"	$6.00-8.00
Plate, Coupe, 8"	$8.00-10.00
Nappie (Round Bowl), 7"	$8.00-10.00
Nappie, 8"	$10.00-12.00
Nappie, 9"	$12.00-14.00
Nappie, 10"	$14.00-16.00
Nappie, 11"	$16.00-18.00
Oatmeal, 6"	$6.00-8.00
Pickle, 8" (Handles)	$12.00-16.00
Salad Covered	$25.00-35.00
Salad Handled	$35.00-45.00
Sauce Boat	$14.00-18.00
Sauce Boat Fast Stand	$16.00-25.00
Sugar, Covered	$16.00-18.00
Teacup	$5.00-7.00
Tea Saucer	$3.00-4.00
Teapot	$65.00-75.00
Jug, 24's, 3⅜ Pint	$35.00-45.00
Egg Cup	$15.00-18.00

REPUBLIC

This list is from the 1927 Homer Laughlin Catalog.

Page 30

Baker, (Oval Bowl) 6"	$6.00-8.00
Baker, 7"	$8.00-12.00
Baker, 8"	$9.00-14.00
Baker, 9"	$10.00-15.00
Baker, 10"	$11.00-16.00
Baker, 11"	$12.00-18.00
Fruits, 5"	$2.00-5.00
Fruits, 6"	$3.00-6.00
Bowl, Deep, 1 Pint	$8.00-12.00
Bowl, Deep, 1⅜ Pint	$15.00-20.00
Oatmeal, 6"	$4.00-8.00
Oatmeal, 6½"	$5.00-9.00
Bone Dish	$15.00-20.00
Butter, Covered	$30.00-40.00
Butter, Individual, 3½"	$5.00-10.00
Cake Plate, 10½"	$16.00-25.00
Covered Dish, 8"	$16.00-20.00
Casserole, Covered	$20.00-35.00
Coffee Cup, AD	$10.00-12.00
Coffee Saucer, AD	$6.00-8.00
Coffee Cup	$8.00-10.00
Coffee Saucer	$3.00-5.00
Cream, ⅝ Pint	$8.00-12.00
Cream, Individual, ½ Pint	$6.00-8.00
Dish, (Platter), 7"	$6.00-10.00
Dish, 9"	$10.00-12.00
Dish, 10"	$11.00-13.00
Dish, 11"	$12.00-14.00
Dish, 12"	$13.00-15.00
Dish, 13"	$14.00-16.00
Dish, 14"	$15.00-18.00
Dish, 15"	$16.00-22.00
Dish, 17"	$18.00-25.00

Jug, 48's, ⅝ Pint	$14.00-18.00
Jug, 42's, 1 Pint	$18.00-24.00
Jug, 36's, 1¾ Pint	$24.00-28.00
Jug, 30's, 2½ Pint	$26.00-30.00
Jug, 24's, 3⅜ Pint	$30.00-32.00
Jug, 12's, 4⅜ Pint	$32.00-36.00
Jug, 6's, 5¾ Pint	$36.00-40.00
Nappie (Round Bowl), 7"	$6.00-8.00
Nappie, 8"	$8.00-12.00
Nappie, 9"	$10.00-15.00
Nappie, 10"	$11.00-16.00
Nappie, 11"	$12.00-18.00
Plate, 6"	$2.00-4.00
Plate, 7"	$3.00-5.00
Plate, 8"	$5.00-7.00
Plate, 9"	$6.00-8.00
Plate, 10"	$8.00-10.00
Plate, Deep, 9"	$8.00-9.00
Plate, Coupe, 7"	$5.00-7.00
Plate, Coupe, 8"	$6.00-8.00
Pickle, 9"	$10.00-12.00
Sauce Boat	$10.00-14.00
Sauce Boat Stand	$4.00-6.00
Oyster Tureen, 8"	$30.00-40.00
Sauce Tureen, 6"	$25.00-35.00
Sauce Tureen Stand, 9"	$10.00-15.00
Ladle	$15.00-20.00
Sugar, 4"	$10.00-15.00
Sugar, Individual, 4"	$8.00-12.00
Teacup	$2.00-5.00
Teapot	$35.00-40.00
Tea Saucer	$1.00-3.00

YELLOWSTONE

This list is from the 1927 Homer Laughlin Catalog.

Page 34

Baker, (Oval Bowl) 5½"	$6.00-10.00
Baker, 8"	$8.00-14.00
Baker, 9"	$10.00-16.00
Baker, 10"	$12.00-18.00
Bowl, Deep, 5"	$8.00-10.00
Bowl, Deep, 6"	$12.00-15.00
Bowl, Oyster, 5"	$12.00-15.00
Bowl, Oyster, 6"	$15.00-20.00
Butter, Covered	$35.00-50.00
Butter, Individual	$6.00-12.00
Cake Plate	$18.00-24.00
Casserole, Covered	$25.00-45.00
Cream Soup	$8.00-10.00
Cream	$8.00-14.00
Cream, Individual	$6.00-12.00
Coffee, AD	$10.00-14.00
Coffee Saucer, AD	$6.00-8.00
Dish, (Platter), 8"	$10.00-14.00
Dish, 10"	$12.00-16.00
Dish, 11"	$14.00-18.00
Dish, 13"	$16.00-20.00
Dish, 15"	$18.00-24.00
Dish, 17"	$20.00-25.00
Oatmeal, 36's	$6.00-8.00
Oatmeal, 30's	$8.00-10.00
Fruits, 5's	$3.00-5.00
Fruits, 6's	$4.00-6.00
Grape Fruits	$10.00-15.00
Jug, 48's	$15.00-20.00
Jug, 36's	$20.00-25.00
Jug, 30's	$25.00-30.00
Jug, 24's	$30.00-35.00
Jug, 12's	$40.00-45.00
Nappie (Round Bowl), 7"	$8.00-12.00
Nappie, 8"	$10.00-14.00
Nappie, 9"	$14.00-16.00
Nappie, 10"	$16.00-20.00
Plate, 5"	$4.00-6.00
Plate, 6"	$5.00-7.00
Plate, 7"	$6.00-8.00
Plate, 8"	$7.00-9.00
Plate, 9"	$8.00-10.00
Plate, Deep, 9"	$8.00-10.00
Plate, Coupe, 7"	$5.00-7.00
Plate, Coupe, 8"	$6.00-7.00
Pickle	$10.00-14.00
Relish	$18.00-20.00
Sauce Boat	$12.00-18.00
Sauce Boat Stand	$5.00-7.00
Fast Stand Sauce Boat	$20.00-30.00
Sugar, Covered	$16.00-20.00
Sugar, Individual	$8.00-14.00
Teacup	$3.00-5.00
Tea Saucer	$2.00-3.00
Teapot	$25.00-40.00

NEWELL/TRELLIS

For Trellis add 50% more.

Pages 44 & 172

Baker, (Oval Bowl) 5½"	$6.00-8.00
Baker, 7"	$8.00-10.00
Baker, 8"	$10.00-12.00
Baker, 9"	$12.00-14.00
Baker, 10"	$14.00-16.00
Bowl, Deep, 1⅛ Pint	$12.00-15.00
Bowl, Deep, 1⅝ Pint	$15.00-20.00
Bowl, Oyster, ¾ Pint	$10.00-12.00
Bowl, Oyster, 1¼ Pint	$15.00-20.00
Boullion Cup, 8 oz.	$10.00-15.00
Boullion Saucer, 6 oz.	$6.00-8.00
Butter, Covered	$50.00-60.00
Butter, Individual, 3"	$6.00-12.00
Cake Plate, 11"	$20.00-25.00
Casserole, Covered	$30.00-35.00
Cream	$8.00-10.00
Dish, (Platter), 8"	$6.00-8.00
Dish, 9"	$10.00-12.00
Dish, 10½"	$12.00-14.00
Dish, 11½"	$14.00-16.00
Dish, 13"	$16.00-20.00
Dish, 15"	$18.00-20.00
Dish, 17"	$20.00-22.00
Fruit, 5"	$4.00-6.00
Fruit, 6"	$6.00-8.00
Jug, 48's, ½ Pint	$15.00-20.00
Jug, 42's, 1 Pint	$20.00-25.00
Jug, 36's, 1½ Pint	$25.00-30.00
Jug, 30's, 2½ Pint	$28.00-32.00
Jug, 24's, 4 Pint	$30.00-35.00
Nappie (Round Bowl), 6"	$6.00-9.00
Nappie, 7"	$7.00-11.00
Nappie, 8"	$8.00-12.00
Nappie, 9"	$12.00-16.00
Oatmeal, 36's, 5"	$6.00-8.00
Oatmeal, 30's, 6"	$8.00-10.00
Plate, 6"	$5.00-7.00
Plate, 7"	$6.00-8.00
Plate, 8"	$7.00-9.00
Plate, 9"	$9.00-11.00
Plate 10"	$10.00-12.00
Plate, Deep, 9"	$7.00-9.00
Plate, Coupe, 7"	$5.00-7.00
Plate, Coupe, 8"	$6.00-8.00
Pickle (Handled)	$10.00-12.00
Sauce Boat	$14.00-18.00
Fast Stand Sauce Boat	$18.00-20.00
Sugar, Covered	$13.00-14.00
Cup, AD	$10.00-12.00
Saucer, AD	$6.00-8.00
Coffee Cup	$10.00-12.00
Coffee Saucer	$6.00-8.00
Teacup	$3.00-5.00
Tea Saucer	$2.00-3.00
Teapot	$40.00-50.00

LIBERTY

Page 50

Baker, (Oval Bowl)	$12.00-16.00
Bowl, 5"	$5.00-6.00
Casserole, Covered	$30.00-40.00
Dish (Platter), 11½"	$10.00-15.00
Dish, 13½"	$12.00-18.00
Dish, 15"	$14.00-20.00
Fruit	$3.50-4.50
Nappy (Round Bowl)	$12.00-16.00
Oatmeal, 6"	$6.00-8.00
Plate, 6"	$3.00-4.00
Plate, 7"	$4.00-5.00
Plate, 8"	$6.00-8.00
Plate, 9"	$6.00-8.00
Plate, 10	$8.00-10.00
Plate, Deep, (Rim Soup)	$7.00-9.00
Pickle	$10.00-12.00
Sauce Boat	$14.00-18.00
Sauce Boat Stand	$8.00-10.00
Sugar, Covered	$12.00-15.00
Creamer,	$7.00-10.00
Teacup	$3.00-6.00
Tea Sacuer	$2.00-4.00
Teapot	$35.00-50.00

VIRGINIA ROSE

Page 56

Baker, (Oval Bowl), 8"	$12.00-18.00
Baker, 9"	$10.00-16.00
Baker, 10"	$12.00-18.00
Bowl, 5" Deep	$8.00-10.00
Casserole, Covered	$45.00-55.00
Covered Butter (Jade)	$65.00-75.00
Dish (Platter), 10½"	$10.00-13.00
Dish, 11½"	$12.00-15.00
Dish, 13"	$13.00-16.00
Dish, 15½"	$20.00-22.00
Double Eggcup (Cable)	$15.00-18.00
Fruit	$3.50-4.50
Nappy (Round Bowl), 8"	$12.00-15.00
Nappy, 9"	$14.00-18.00
Nappy, 10"	$15.00-20.00
Oatmeal, 6"	$5.00-6.00
Plate, 6"	$5.00-6.00
Plate, 7"	$4.00-5.00
Plate, 8"	$8.00-10.00
Plate, 9"	$5.00-6.00
Plate, 10"	$8.00-10.00
Plate, Deep (Rim Soup)	$6.00-8.00
Coupe Soup	$8.00-10.00
Cream Soup	$12.00-14.00
Cream Soup Saucer	$6.00-8.00
Onion Soup (Lug)	$10.00-12.00
Cake Plate	$13.00-18.00
Pickle	$8.00-10.00
Sauce Boat	$12.00-18.00
Sauce Boat Stand	$10.00-12.00
Fast Stand Sauce Boat	$16.00-20.00
Teacup	$4.00-5.00
Tea Saucer	$2.00-3.00
Cup, AD	$10.00-12.00
Saucer, AD	$6.00-8.00
Coffee Mug	$16.00-20.00
Sugar, Covered	$12.00-15.00
Cream	$8.00-10.00
Shakers (Swing)	$40.00-50.00
Shakers (KK)	$40.00-50.00
Tray With Handles	$20.00-25.00
Jug, 5"	$20.00-25.00
Jug, 7½"	$65.00-75.00
Jug, Covered, 5"	$50.00-60.00
Jug, Covered, 7½"	$95.00-105.00

MARIGOLD

Page 62

Baker, (Oval Bowl).....................$15.00-20.00	Plate, 9".......................................$8.00-10.00
Bowl, 5"...$6.00-8.00	Plate, 10"....................................$10.00-12.00
Bowl, 6"...$8.00-10.00	Plate, Deep (Rim Soup).................$6.00-8.00
Casserole, Covered...................$30.00-40.00	Cream Soup $16.00-18.00
Dish (Platter), 11".....................$12.00-16.00	Cream Soup Saucer $10.00-12.00
Dish, 13"....................................$16.00-20.00	Milk Pitcher $25.00-35.00
Dish, 15"....................................$18.00-25.00	Sauce Boat.................................$16.00-20.00
Fruit..$3.00-5.00	Sauce Boat Stand......................$10.00-12.00
Nappy (Round Bowl), 9"...........$15.00-20.00	Sugar, Covered $14.00-18.00
Plate, 6"...$4.00-5.00	Cream...$10.00-15.00
Plate, 7"...$5.00-6.00	Teacup $3.50-4.50
Plate, 8"...$6.00-8.00	Tea Saucer $2.00-3.00
Plate, 8" Square..........................$8.00-10.00	

WELLS

Page 68

Baker, (Oval Bowl), 9"	$15.00-20.00
Bowl, Deep, 5"	$12.00-15.00
Bowl, Deep, 6"	$14.00-18.00
Casserole, Covered	$35.00-45.00
Dish, (Platter), 11"	$15.00-18.00
Dish, 13"	$18.00-20.00
Dish, 15"	$22.00-25.00
Fruit	$4.00-5.00
Nappy (Round Bowl), 9"	$15.00-20.00
Plate, 6"	$4.00-5.00
Plate, 7"	$6.00-7.00
Plate, 8"	$7.00-8.00
Plate, 8", Square	$12.50-15.00
Plate, 9"	$10.00-12.00
Plate, 10"	$12.00-14.00
Muffin Cover	$45.00-50.00
Double Eggcup	$12.00-16.00
Plate, Deep (Rim Soup)	$7.00-10.00
Cream Soup	$12.00-16.00
Cream Soup Saucer	$6.00-8.00
Chop Plate	$18.00-24.00
Pickle (Handles)	$10.00-14.00
Sauce Boat	$14.00-20.00
Sauce Boat Stand	$8.00-10.00
Sugar, Covered	$14.00-18.00
Cream	$10.00-14.00
Teacup	$3.00-5.00
Tea Saucer	$2.00-4.00
Cup, AD	$10.00-15.00
Saucer, AD	$6.00-8.00
Coffee Pot, AD	$25.00-30.00
Teapot	$40.00-50.00
Jug, Covered 42's	$25.00-30.00
Jug, Covered, 24's	$40.00-50.00

CENTURY

Page 72

Baker, (Oval Bowl), 8"	$12.00-18.00
Baker, 9"	$14.00-20.00
Bowl, Deep, 1 Pint	$15.00-20.00
Bowl, Oyster, 1 Pint	$20.00-25.00
Butter, (Century)	$75.00-85.00
Butter, (Jade)	$50.00-60.00
Casserole, Covered	$50.00-70.00
Double Egg Cup	$15.00-20.00
Fruit	$3.00-4.00
Dish, (Platter), 10"	$10.00-14.00
Dish, (Oval Well), 11"	$14.00-18.00
Dish, (Sq. Well), 11"	$12.00-16.00
Dish, (Oval Well), 13"	$16.00-20.00
Dish, (Sq. Well), 13"	$14.00-18.00
Dish, 15"	$18.00-25.00
Dish, (Platter), Sq.	$25.00-35.00
Jug, ⅝ Pint	$25.00-30.00
Jug, 2½ Pint	$30.00-35.00
Jug, Covered ⅝ Pint	$40.00-45.00
Jug, Covered 2½ Pint	$50.00-55.00
Muffin Cover	$45.00-50.00
Nappy, 7"	$10.00-15.00
Nappy, 8"	$14.00-18.00
Nappy, 9"	$15.00-20.00
Oatmeal, 6"	$10.00-12.00
Plate, 6"	$3.00-4.00
Plate, 7"	$5.00-7.00
Plate, 8"	$7.00-9.00
Plate, 9"	$9.00-11.00
Plate, 10"	$12.00-15.00
Cake Plate, 11½"	$15.00-20.00
Plate, Deep, (Rim Soup)	$8.00-10.00
Cream Soup Cup, 11 oz.	$15.00-20.00
Cream Soup Saucer	$10.00-12.00
Onion Soup (Lug)	$8.00-10.00
Sauce Boat	$15.00-20.00
Sauce Boat Stand	$16.00-20.00
Fast Stand Sauce Boat	$20.00-25.00
Sugar, Covered	$14.00-16.00
Creamer	$10.00-12.00
Teacup	$4.00-6.00
Tea Saucer	$2.00-4.00
Cup, AD	$10.00-15.00
Saucer, AD	$8.00-10.00
Coffee Cup	$10.00-15.00
Coffee Saucer	$8.00-10.00
Teapot	$60.00-75.00

NAUTILUS

Page 78

Baker, (Oval Bowl), 9"	$12.00-16.00	Plate, 10"	$7.00-9.00
Baker, 10"	$14.00-18.00	Plate, Deep, (Rim Soup)	$6.00-8.00
Bowl, 5" (36's)	$6.00-8.00	Coupe Soup	$6.00-8.00
Bowl, 6" (30's)	$8.00-10.00	Onion Soup (Lug)	$8.00-10.00
Casserole, Covered	$35.00-45.00	Oatmeal, 6"	$5.00-8.00
Covered Butter, (Jade)	$40.00-50.00	Sauce Boat	$16.00-20.00
Dish (Platter)10"	$10.00-15.00	Sauce Boat Stand	$6.00-8.00
Dish, 12"	$12.00-18.00	Sugar, Covered	$12.00-18.00
Dish, 14"	$16.00-22.00	Cream	$10.00-16.00
Fruit	$3.00-6.00	Teacup	$3.50-4.50
Nappy (Round Bowl), 9"	$12.00-16.00	Tea Saucer	$2.00-3.00
Nappy, 10"	$14.00-18.00	Cup, AD	$10.00-15.00
Plate, 6"	$3.00-5.00	Saucer, AD	$5.00-8.00
Plate, 7"	$5.00-7.00	Double Eggcup (Cable)	$12.00-16.00
Plate, 8" (Rare)	$10.00-12.00	Baltimore Coffee Mug	$15.00-20.00
Plate, 9"	$6.00-8.00		

CORONET

Page 88

Baker, (Oval Bowl).....................$15.00-25.00
Bowl, 5" $6.00-8.00
Casserole, Covered...................$45.00-50.00
Dish (Platter), 11" $12.00-16.00
Dish, 13".................................$16.00-20.00
Dish, 15".................................$22.00-25.00
Fruit.......................................$4.00-6.00
Nappy (Round Bowl)................$15.00-25.00
Plate, 6" $4.00-6.00
Plate, 7" $5.00-7.00
Plate, 8" $7.00-9.00

Plate, 9" $9.00-12.00
Plate, 10"................................$11.00-15.00
Plate, Deep, (Rim Soup)..............$8.00-10.00
Pickle.....................................$10.00-14.00
Sauce Boat...............................$18.00-20.00
Sauce Boat Stand $8.00-10.00
Sugar, Covered $15.00-20.00
Cream.....................................$9.00-15.00
Teacup $4.00-6.00
Tea Saucer $3.00-4.00

BRITTANY/PICCADILLY

Picadilly is priced the same as regular Brittany.
The Brittany Nappy Cover in the 10" and the Double Eggcup were not made in the silk screen patterns.

Pages 92 & 100

Bowl, Deep, 5" $8.00-10.00
Bowl, Deep, 6" $10.00-12.00
Casserole, Covered....................$25.00-35.00
Dish, (Platter), 11" $10.00-16.00
Dish, 13" $12.00-18.00
Dish, 15" $15.00-20.00
Double Eggcup, (Cable) $12.00-15.00
Fruit...$2.00-4.00
Nappy, 10" $12.00-16.00
Plate, 6" $4.00-6.00
Plate, 7" $5.00-7.00
Plate, 8" $6.00-8.00
Plate, 9" $7.00-9.00

Plate, 10"......................................$8.00-10.00
Chop Plate, 13".........................$18.00-25.00
Plate, Deep (Rim Soup)................$6.00-8.00
Cream Soup $8.00-10.00
Cream Soup Saucer $6.00-8.00
Pickle...$6.00-8.00
Sauce Boat $12.00-18.00
Sauce Boat Stand $6.00-8.00
Sugar, Covered $10.00-14.00
Cream...$8.00-12.00
Teacup $2.50-5.00
Tea Saucer $1.50-3.00
Teapot $30.00-40.00

EGGSHELL NAUTILUS

Page 104

Baker, 9"	$12.00-14.00	Onion soup (Lug)	$6.00-8.00
Baker, 10"	$14.00-16.00	Cream Soup	$8.00-10.00
Bowl, 5"	$6.00-8.00	Cream Soup Saucer	$5.00-6.00
Casserole, Covered	$20.00-35.00	Chop Plate, 14"	$16.00-20.00
Dish, (Platter), 11"	$10.00-15.00	Pickle	$6.00-8.00
Dish, 13"	$12.00-18.00	Sauce Boat	$14.00-18.00
Dish, 15"	$14.00-20.00	Sauce Boat Stand	$6.00-8.00
Fruit	$4.00-6.00	Fast Stand Sauce Boat	$16.00-20.00
Nappy, 9"	$12.00-14.00	Sugar, Covered	$12.00-14.00
Nappy, 10"	$14.00-16.00	Cream	$8.00-10.00
Oatmeal, 6"	$8.00-10.00	Shakers, (Swing)	$12.00-15.00
Plate, 6"	$3.00-4.00	Teacup	$2.00-4.00
Plate, 7"	$4.00-5.00	Teacup Saucer	$1.50-3.00
Plate, 8"	$6.00-8.00	Cup, AD, (Swing)	$8.00-12.00
Plate, 8" Square	$6.00-8.00	Saucer, AD, (Swing)	$4.00-6.00
Palte, 9"	$7.00-8.00	Teapot	$35.00-45.00
Plate, 10"	$8.00-10.00	Double Eggcup, (Swing)	$12.00-14.00
Plate, Deep, (Rim Soup)	$6.00-8.00		

EGGSHELL GEORGIAN

For Craftsman or Regular Georgian add 15% more.

Page 116

Baker, 9"	$12.00-15.00
Baker, 10"	$14.00-18.00
Bowl, 5"	$6.00-8.00
Casserole, Covered	$20.00-40.00
Dish, (Platter), 11"	$12.00-15.00
Dish, 13"	$14.00-18.00
Dish, 15"	$16.00-25.00
Fruit	$3.00-5.00
Nappy, 9"	$12.00-15.00
Nappy, 10"	$14.00-18.00
Oatmeal, 6"	$6.00-8.00
Plate, 6"	$3.00-5.00
Plate, 7"	$4.00-6.00
Plate, 8"	$6.00-8.00
Plate, 8" Square	$8.00-10.00
Palte, 9"	$7.00-9.00
Plate, 10"	$8.00-11.00
Plate, Deep, (Rim Soup)	$6.00-8.00

Onion soup (Lug)	$8.00-10.00
Cream Soup	$8.00-10.00
Cream Soup Saucer	$6.00-8.00
Chop Plate, 14"	$15.00-25.00
Pickle	$6.00-8.00
Sauce Boat	$14.00-18.00
Sauce Boat Stand	$6.00-8.00
Fast Stand Sauce Boat	$16.00-20.00
Sugar, Covered	$14.00-16.00
Cream	$10.00-12.00
Shakers	$16.00-20.00
Teacup	$2.00-4.00
Teacup Saucer	$1.50-2.50
Cup, AD	$8.00-12.00
Saucer, AD	$6.00-10.00
Teapot	$40.00-50.00
Double Eggcup	$12.00-15.00

SWING

Page 126

Baker, (Oval Bowl)	$12.00-18.00
Butter Dish	$40.00-50.00
Casserole, Covered	$25.00-35.00
Dish, (Platter), 11"	$12.00-18.00
Dish, 13"	$14.00-20.00
Dish, 15"	$16.00-24.00
Fruit	$2.00-3.00
Nappy (Round Bowl)	$12.00-18.00
Oatmeal	$5.00-8.00
Plate, 6"	$4.00-5.00
Plate, 7"	$6.00-8.00
Plate, 8"	$7.00-9.00
Plate, 9"	$8.00-10.00
Plate, 10"	$10.00-12.00
Double Eggcup	$8.00-14.00
Plate, Deep (Rim Soup)	$6.00-8.00
Soup Saucer	$5.00-6.00
Sauce Boat	$12.00-18.00
Sauce Boat Stand	$6.00-8.00
Shakers	$10.00-15.00
Sugar, Covered	$12.00-16.00
Cream	$12.00-14.00
Teacup	$3.00-5.00
Tea Saucer	$2.00-3.00
Sugar, AD	$6.00-15.00
Cream, AD	$4.00-12.00
Cup, AD	$10.00-18.00
Saucer, AD	$4.00-6.00
Coffee Pot	$16.00-30.00
Muffin Cover	$16.00-30.00

THEME

Page 134

Baker, 9"	$15.00-18.00
Casserole, Covered	$25.00-40.00
Dish, (Platter), 10"	$14.00-16.00
Dish, 12"	$16.00-18.00
Dish, 14"	$18.00-20.00
Fruit	$3.00-4.00
Nappy, 9"	$15.00-18.00
Plate, 6"	$3.00-4.00
Plate, 7"	$5.00-6.00
Plate, 8", Square	$7.00-9.00
Plate, 9"	$7.00-9.00
Plate, 10"	$8.00-10.00
Plate, Deep, (Rim Soup)	$6.00-8.00
Onion Soup, (Lug)	$10.00-12.00
Cream Soup	$10.00-15.00
Cream Soup Saucer	6.00-8.00
Chop Plate, 14"	$20.00-30.00
Pickle	$6.00-8.00
Sauce Boat	$12.00-16.00
Sauce Boat Stand	$6.00-8.00
Fast Stand Sauce Boat	$14.00-18.00
Sugar, Covered	$12.00-16.00
Cream	$10.00-12.00
Teacup	$3.00-4.00
Teacup Saucer	$2.00-3.00
Cup, AD	$10.00-14.00
Saucer, AD	$6.00-8.00
Shakers	$15.00-20.00
Teapot	$40.00-50.00

DEBUTANTE

Suntone is 20% more; Skytone is 15% more.

Page 138

Casserole, Covered	$25.00-30.00
Dish, (Platter), 11"	$12.00-16.00
Dish, 13"	$16.00-20.00
Dish, 15"	$18.00-25.00
Chop Plate, 15"	$16.00-20.00
Double Eggcup	$10.00-15.00
Fruit	$3.00-5.00
Nappy, 9"	$10.00-14.00
Nappy, 10"	$12.00-16.00
Plate, 6"	$3.00-4.00
Plate, 7"	$5.00-6.00
Plate, 9"	$7.00-8.00
Plate, 10"	$8.00-9.00

Coupe Soup	$5.00-6.00
Onion Soup (Lug)	$6.00-8.00
Pie Server	$20.00-30.00
Fast Stand Sauce Boat	$15.00-20.00
Shakers	$10.00-15.00
Sugar, Covered	$12.00-18.00
Cream	$10.00-14.00
Teacup	$3.00-5.00
Tea Saucer	$2.00-3.00
Cup, AD	$10.00-12.00
Saucer, AD	$4.00-6.00
Teapot	$35.00-45.00
Coffee Pot	$45.00-55.00

CAVALIER

The Cavalier AD cup was listed as having a special handle.

Page 146

Casserole, Covered	$20.00-30.00
Cereal/Soup (Charm House)	$5.00-9.00
Fruit	$3.00-4.00
Dish, (Platter), 11"	$10.00-14.00
Dish, 13"	$12.00-16.00
Dish, 15"	$16.00-20.00
Nappy, (Round Bowl), 9"	$10.00-15.00
Plate, 6"	$3.00-6.00
Plate, 7"	$4.00-7.00
Plate, Square, 8"	$6.00-9.00
Plate, 9"	$6.00-9.00
Sauce Boat	$14.00-18.00
Shakers, (Jubilee Shape)	$8.00-10.00
Sugar, Covered	$12.00-15.00
Cream	$8.00-12.00
Teacup	$3.00-5.00
Tea Saucer	$2.00-4.00
Cup, AD (Jubilee Shape)	$10.00-12.00
Saucer, AD (Swing)	$6.00-8.00
Teapot	$20.00-35.00

RHYTHM

Page 156

Cereal/Soup, 5½"	$5.00-7.00	Sauce Boat	$8.00-12.00
Coupe Soup	$6.00-8.00	Sauce Boat Stand	$3.00-5.00
Fruit	$3.00-4.00	Fast Stand Sauce Boat	$12.00-16.00
Nappy, (Round Bowl)	$10.00-15.00	Shakers (Swing)	$10.00-15.00
Dish, (Platter), 11½"	$12.00-16.00	Spoon Rest	$80.00-100.00
Dish, 13½"	$14.00-18.00	Sugar, Covered	$10.00-14.00
Dish, 15½"	$16.00-25.00	Cream	$8.00-10.00
Jug, 2 Quarts	$15.00-20.00	Teacup	$3.00-4.00
Plate, 6"	$3.00-5.00	Tea Saucer	$2.00-3.00
Plate, 7"	$5.00-6.00	Cup, AD	$8.00-10.00
Plate, 8"	$6.00-7.00	Saucer, AD	$4.00-6.00
Plate, 9"	$7.00-8.00	Teapot	$35.00-45.00
Plate, 10"	$8.00-9.00	Tid-Bit Tray	$20.00-30.00
Casserole, Covered	$30.00-40.00		

DURAPRINT

Duraprint flatware is Rhythm, as is the sauce boat. The other hollowware is Charm House.

Page 162

Cereal/Soup, 5½"	$4.00-6.00
Coupe Soup	$4.00-7.00
Fruit	$2.00-5.00
Dish, (Platter), 11½"	$10.00-12.00
Dish, 13½"	$12.00-15.00
Dish, 15½"	$14.00-18.00
Casserole, (Charm House)	$25.00-30.00
Plate, 6"	$3.00-6.00
Plate, 7"	$4.00-7.00
Plate, 8"	$5.00-8.00
Plate, 9"	$6.00-9.00
Plate, 10"	$7.00-10.00
Sauce Boat	$8.00-12.00
Sauce Boat Stand	$4.00-7.00
Shakers, (Charm House)	$10.00-15.00
Teapot, (Charm House)	$30.00-40.00
Sugar, (Charm House)	$10.00-18.00
Cream, (Charm House)	$7.00-14.00
Teacup, (Charm House)	$3.00-5.00
Tea Saucer (Charm House)	$2.00-4.00
Ashtray	$15.00-20.00
Tiered Tid-bit Tray	$30.00-40.00

JADE

Items are from drawings found at Homer Laughlin.

Page 166

Baker, (Oval Bowl)	$15.00-20.00		Plate, Deep (Rim Soup)	$8.00-10.00
Bowl, Deep, 36's	$12.00-15.00		Plate, 10"	$12.00-15.00
Cake Plate	$30.00-40.00		Cream Soup	$12.00-16.00
Casserole, Covered	$35.00-45.00		Cream Soup Saucer	$8.00-10.00
Covered Butter	$40.00-50.00		Sauce Boat	$18.00-20.00
Dish, (Platter), 11"	$18.00-20.00		Sauce Boat Stand	$8.00-10.00
Dish, 13"	$20.00-24.00		Fast Stand Sauce Boat	$22.00-25.00
Dish, 15"	$25.00-30.00		Sugar, Covered	$16.00-20.00
Fruit	$6.00-8.00		Cream	$12.00-15.00
Jug	$30.00-40.00		Teacup	$6.00-8.00
Nappy, (Round Bowl)	$16.00-20.00		Tea Saucer	$4.00-5.00
Oatmeal, 36's	$8.00-10.00		Coffee Cup	$15.00-20.00
Plate, 6"	$5.00-7.00		Coffee Saucer	$10.00-12.00
Plate, 7"	$6.00-9.00		Cup, AD	$15.00-20.00
Plate, 8"	$7.00-10.00		Saucer, AD	$10.00-12.00
Plate, 9"	$9.00-11.00		Teapot	$50.00-60.00

ORLEANS

Items listed are from drawings found at Homer Laughlin.

Page 168

Baker, (Oval Bowl), 8" $15.00-18.00
Baker, 9" $18.00-20.00
Bowl, 5" $6.00-8.00
Casserole, Covered..................$35.00-45.00
Dish, (Platter), 11" $14.00-16.00
Dish, 13" $18.00-20.00
Dish, 15" $22.00-25.00
Fruit..$5.00-7.00
Nappy, (Round Bowl), 9" $16.00-18.00
Oatmeal, 6" $8.00-10.00
Plate, 6" $4.00-5.00
Plate, 7" $6.00-8.00

Plate, 8" $8.00-10.00
Plate, 9" $12.00-14.00
Plate, 10" $13.00-15.00
Plate, Deep, (Rim Soup).............$8.00-10.00
Pickle...$10.00-12.00
Sauce Boat $18.00-20.00
Sauce Boat Stand $10.00-12.00
Sugar, Open $14.00-18.00
Cream..$12.00-16.00
Teacup $5.00-6.00
Tea Saucer $3.00-4.00
Teapot $75.00-85.00

RAVENNA

Items listed are from drawings found at Homer Laughlin.

Page 170

Baker, (Oval Bowl)	$16.00-18.00	Plate, 8"	$8.00-10.00
Bowl, Deep, 5"	$8.00-10.00	Plate, 9"	$10.00-12.00
Casserole, Covered	$30.00-40.00	Plate, 10"	$12.00-14.00
Dish, (Platter), 11"	$14.00-18.00	Plate, Deep, (Rim Soup)	$8.00-10.00
Dish, 13"	$18.00-20.00	Sauce Boat	$18.00-20.00
Dish, 15"	$20.00-25.00	Sauce Boat Stand	$10.00-12.00
Fruit	$5.00-7.00	Sugar, Open	$14.00-16.00
Nappy, (Round Bowl)	$16.00-18.00	Sugar, Covered	$16.00-20.00
Oatmeal, 6"	$8.00-10.00	Cream	$12.00-14.00
Plate, 6"	$5.00-6.00	Teacup	$5.00-6.00
Plate, 7"	$6.00-8.00	Tea Saucer	$3.00-4.00

Books on Antiques and Collectibles

Most of the following books are available from your local book seller or antique dealer, or on loan from your public library. If you are unable to locate certain titles in your area you may order by mail from COLLECTOR BOOKS, P.O. Box 3009, Paducah, KY 42002-3009. This is only a partial listing of the books on antiques that are available from Collector Books. All books are well illustrated and contain current values. Add $2.00 for postage for the first book ordered and $.30 for each additional book. Include item number, title and price when ordering. Allow 14 to 21 days for delivery.

BOOKS ON GLASS AND POTTERY

1810	American Art Glass, Shuman	$29.95
2016	Bedroom & Bathroom Glassware of the Depression Years	$19.95
1312	Blue & White Stoneware, McNerney	$9.95
1959	Blue Willow, 2nd Ed., Gaston	$14.95
2270	Collectible Glassware from the 40's, 50's, & 60's, Florence	$19.95
3311	Collecting Yellow Ware - Id. & Value Gd., McAllister	$16.95
2352	Collector's Ency. of Akro Agate Glassware, Florence	$14.95
1373	Collector's Ency. of American Dinnerware, Cunningham	$24.95
2272	Collector's Ency. of California Pottery, Chipman	$24.95
3312	Collector's Ency. of Children's Dishes, Whitmyer	$19.95
2133	Collector's Ency. of Cookie Jars, Roerig	$24.95
2273	Collector's Ency. of Depression Glass, 10th Ed., Florence	$19.95
2209	Collector's Ency. of Fiesta, 7th Ed., Huxford	$19.95
1439	Collector's Ency. of Flow Blue China, Gaston	$19.95
1915	Collector's Ency. of Hall China, 2nd Ed., Whitmyer	$19.95
2334	Collector's Ency. of Majolica Pottery, Katz-Marks	$19.95
1358	Collector's Ency. of McCoy Pottery, Huxford	$19.95
3313	Collector's Ency. of Niloak, Gifford	$19.95
1039	Collector's Ency. of Nippon Porcelain I, Van Patten	$19.95
2089	Collector's Ency. of Nippon Porcelain II, Van Patten	$24.95
1665	Collector's Ency. of Nippon Porcelain III, Van Patten	$24.95
1034	Collector's Ency. of Roseville Pottery, Huxford	$19.95
1035	Collector's Ency. of Roseville Pottery, 2nd Ed., Huxford	$19.95
3314	Collector's Ency. of Van Briggle Art Pottery, Sasicki	$24.95
2339	Collector's Guide to Shawnee Pottery, Vanderbilt	$19.95
1425	Cookie Jars, Westfall	$9.95
2275	Czechoslovakian Glass & Collectibles, Barta	$16.95
3315	Elegant Glassware of the Depression Era, 5th Ed., Florence	$19.95
3318	Glass Animals of the Depression Era, Garmon & Spencer	$19.95
2024	Kitchen Glassware of the Depression Years, 4th Ed., Florence	$19.95
2379	Lehner's Ency. of U.S. Marks on Pottery, Porcelain & Clay	$24.95
2394	Oil Lamps II, Thuro	$24.95
3322	Pocket Guide to Depression Glass, 8th Ed., Florence	$9.95
2345	Portland Glass, Ladd	$24.95
1670	Red Wing Collectibles, DePasquale	$9.95
1440	Red Wing Stoneware, DePasquale	$9.95
1958	So. Potteries Blue Ridge Dinnerware, 3rd Ed., Newbound	$14.95
2221	Standard Carnival Glass, 3rd Ed., Edwards	$24.95
1848	Very Rare Glassware of the Depression Years, Florence	$24.95
2140	Very Rare Glassware of the Depression Years, Second Series	$24.95
3326	Very Rare Glassware of the Depression Era, Third Series	$24.95
3327	Watt Pottery - Identification & Value Guide, Morris	$19.95
2224	World of Salt Shakers, 2nd Ed., Lechner	$24.95

BOOKS ON DOLLS & TOYS

2079	Barbie Fashion, Vol. 1, 1959-1967, Eames	$24.95
3310	Black Dolls - 1820-1991 - Id. & Value Guide, Perkins	$17.95
1514	Character Toys & Collectibles 1st Series, Longest	$19.95
1750	Character Toys & Collectibles, 2nd Series, Longest	$19.95
1529	Collector's Ency. of Barbie Dolls, DeWein	$19.95
2338	Collector's Ency. of Disneyana, Longest & Stern	$24.95
2342	Madame Alexander Price Guide #17, Smith	$9.95
1540	Modern Toys, 1930-1980, Baker	$19.95
2343	Patricia Smith's Doll Values Antique to Modern, 8th ed	$12.95
1886	Stern's Guide to Disney	$14.95

2139	Stern's Guide to Disney, 2nd Series	$14.95
1513	Teddy Bears & Steiff Animals, Mandel	$9.95
1817	Teddy Bears & Steiff Animals, 2nd, Mandel	$19.95
2084	Teddy Bears, Annalees & Steiff Animals, 3rd, Mandel	$19.95
2028	Toys, Antique & Collectible, Longest	$14.95
1808	Wonder of Barbie, Manos	$9.95
1430	World of Barbie Dolls, Manos	$9.95

OTHER COLLECTIBLES

1457	American Oak Furniture, McNerney	$9.95
2269	Antique Brass & Copper, Gaston	$16.95
2333	Antique & Collectible Marbles, 3rd Ed., Grist,	$9.95
1712	Antique & Collectible Thimbles, Mathis	$19.95
1748	Antique Purses, Holiner	$19.95
1868	Antique Tools, Our American Heritage, McNerney	$9.95
1426	Arrowheads & Projectile Points, Hothem	$7.95
1278	Art Nouveau & Art Deco Jewelry, Baker	$9.95
1714	Black Collectibles, Gibbs	$19.95
1128	Bottle Pricing Guide, 3rd Ed., Cleveland	$7.95
1751	Christmas Collectibles, Whitmyer	$19.95
1752	Christmas Ornaments, Johnston	$19.95
2132	Collector's Ency. of American Furniture, Vol. I, Swedberg	$24.95
2271	Collector's Ency. of American Furniture, Vol. II, Swedberg	$24.95
2018	Collector's Ency. of Graniteware, Greguire	$24.95
2083	Collector's Ency. of Russel Wright Designs, Kerr	$19.95
2337	Collector's Guide to Decoys, Book II, Huxford	$16.95
2340	Collector's Guide to Easter Collectibles, Burnett	$16.95
1441	Collector's Guide to Post Cards, Wood	$9.95
2276	Decoys, Kangas	$24.95
1629	Doorstops, Id. & Values, Bertoia	$9.95
1716	Fifty Years of Fashion Jewelry, Baker	$19.95
3316	Flea Market Trader, 8th Ed., Huxford	$9.95
3317	Florence's Standard Baseball Card Price Gd., 5th Ed.	$9.95
1755	Furniture of the Depression Era, Swedberg	$19.95
1424	Hatpins & Hatpin Holders, Baker	$9.95
3319	Huxford's Collectible Advertising - Id. & Value Gd.	$17.95
1181	100 Years of Collectible Jewelry, Baker	$9.95
2023	Keen Kutter Collectibles, 2nd Ed., Heuring	$14.95
2216	Kitchen Antiques - 1790-1940, McNerney	$14.95
3320	Modern Guns - Id. & Val. Gd., 9th Ed., Quertermous	$12.95
1965	Pine Furniture, Our Am. Heritage, McNerney	$14.95
3321	Ornamental & Figural Nutcrackers, Rittenhouse	$16.95
2026	Railroad Collectibles, 4th Ed., Baker	$14.95
1632	Salt & Pepper Shakers, Guarnaccia	$9.95
1888	Salt & Pepper Shakers II, Guarnaccia	$14.95
2220	Salt & Pepper Shakers III, Guarnaccia	$14.95
3323	Schroeder's Antique Price Guide, 11th Ed.	$12.95
3324	Schroeder's Antique & Coll. 1993 Engag. Calendar	$9.95
2346	Sheet Music Ref. & Price Guide, Pafik & Guiheen	$18.95
2096	Silverplated Flatware, 4th Ed., Hagan	$14.95
3325	Standard Knife Collector's Guide, Stewart	$12.95
2348	20th Century Fashionable Plastic Jewelry, Baker	$19.95
2349	Value Guide to Baseball Collectibles, Raycraft	$16.95

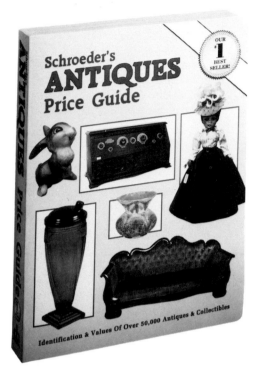